contents

Editorials ....
Reviews ....
Interviews 35
  • Daniel Stamm 37
  • Marcus Dunstan 43
Articles 49
  • Adventures in Porno Land 50
  • The Peculiar Pornography of 57
    Mario Siciliano
  • Six Head-Slapping Shark Tales 63
  • Taking **TUSK** on its own Terms 71
  • Dirty Uncle Jimbo's Top Ten 76
  • Family-Friendly Halloween Films 84
  • The Films of Nikos Nikolaidis 91
  • Steve's Video Store Halloween 103
Bookshelf 107
Contributors 108

Wrap Around Cover Art: Joe Deagnon

Interior Art: Heather Paxton (page 1), David Reddick (page 47), Salvatore Tarantola (page 70), Jill Thompson (page 83)

Random Jack-o'-lantern photos: Tony Strauss

Brian Harris, Editor & Publisher • **Timothy Paxton**, Editor & Lay Out/Design
Tony Strauss, Editor & Proofing • **Steve Fenton**, Assistant Editor

WENG'S CHOP Halloween Special Edition is printed annually. © 2014 Wildside Publishing / Kronos Productions. All rights reserved. No part of this publication may be reproduced, distributed, or transmitted in any form or by any means, including photocopying, recording, or other electronic or mechanical methods, without the prior written permission of the publisher, except in the case of brief quotations embodied in critical reviews and certain other noncommercial uses permitted by copyright law. For permission requests, write to the publisher, addressed "Attention: Permissions Coordinator," at the address below.
4301 Sioux Lane #1, McHenry, IL 60050, United States
wengschop@comcast.net
Volume #2 / Issue #6.5 / 1st Printing

WHAT WE SAID...

PUTTING THE "LOW" BACK IN HALLOWEEN

HAPPY FREAKIN' HALLOWEEN (give or take a few damn days depending on when this issue is released), *READERS!* So, can you believe the goddamn ass-kicking coming out of Wildside/Kronos Publications this year? Seriously! We're on issue #10 of Tim Paxton's *Monster!* digest and #6.5 of *Weng's Chop* magazine (this issue here), and we've still got more in store for readers this year including *Monster!* digest issues #11 and #12, *Weng's Chop* magazine #7, *Monster! International* #1 and *Art by Heather: The Halloween Pumpkin Digest* (our first full-color publication, this latter is now available at *wengschopstore.com* and Amazon)! What do we have lined up for 2015? I know we'll see another dozen or so issues of *Monster!*, at least four issues of *Weng's Chop*, a few digest-sized one-shots, a Kindle version of *filmBRAWL* and god knows what else. Major props to all of our writers and extra special thanks to compadres Tim Paxton, Tony Strauss and Steve Fenton for helping make every month something for film fans to look forward to! So enough about us, let's talk about me and how wonderful I am...

HALLOWEEN RESOLUTIONS: BRING BACK THE HORROR HOLIDAY!

We all know most of us don't follow through with New Year's Eve resolutions intended to cover an entire year; most are just outlandish and often impossible. So I decided to make resolutions for a single day, to be followed as faithfully as I can for the rest of my life, that will not only improve Halloween for me and mine, but also you and yours.

- I will watch **HALLOWEEN III: SEASON OF THE WITCH** every single day during the month of October. (2015 only)
- I will go balls-out, purchasing an insanely expensive and terrifying mask.
- I will do my best to scare at least one child off my porch. Especially the ones dressed as Moses, Noah and Roman soldiers.
- I will only give gross, offensive candy to the trick 'r treaters.
- I will learn how to make sugar skulls, so I can give them to friends as Halloween gifts.
- I will make every single Halloween memorable in some way for my youngest child, whether that's with crafts, baking or pumpkin carving.
- I will perform a single prank.

India's first pumpkin carving (left); Daddy's on the right

So there you have it, my Halloween resolutions. How about you, do you have any resolutions you'd like to make for Halloween? Whatever they may be, I hope they're wicked fun!

Before I leave you to the book in your hands, please be sure to check out the Facebook group World Wide Horror (*facebook.com/groups/worldwidehorror/*) for horror/exploitation film news and discussions from around the world, as well as sneak peeks of upcoming covers and special Wildside/Kronos Publications giveaways!

~ *Brian Harris, co-editor*

LET'S REANIMATE THIS CORPSE

Welcome back, *Chop*pers, to our second Spooktacular Special! I hope y'all had a spooktacularly frightful and fun-filled Halloween this year! What did you dress as? I didn't have much time to put together too fancy of a costume, so I had to go with my old standby: registered sex offender on house arrest (with actual, working ankle tracking bracelet). But as we all know, Halloween isn't about *what* we dress as…it's about *how* we use candy to lure children to our front door, and I think it's important to remember that on this special holiday.

Speaking of which, with all inappropriate kidding aside, I don't know about y'all, but we had an alarmingly low number of trick-or-treaters roaming the neighborhood this year, continuing the downward trend that we've seen over the past few Halloweens. Each year, there seem to be fewer and fewer trick-or-treaters. I don't know if it's that kids don't consider Halloween cool anymore (hard to believe; playing dress-up and collecting free candy pretty much sells itself), or if it's the fact that so many people nowadays turn off their porch lights and hide from the holiday like a bunch of sourpuss poopyheads.

I'm betting that it's the latter reason. We live on a cul-de-sac of about 20 houses, and including ours, there were only three houses with their porch lights on to indicate their holiday participation.

Three.

Are you fucking kidding me, people?

Okay, we need to have a serious talk here. I don't know who the hell told you that you get to just beg off from Halloween, but whoever it was was completely full of shit. You don't just beg off from Halloween.

This is what is known as a dick move.

You're being dicks.

What you do on Halloween—I don't care who you are—is you buy some fucking candy and you turn your fucking porch light on and you goddam well put a fucking smile on your face and hand out candy to the kids who come to your door. You compliment their costumes that they're wearing, and you wish them a happy Halloween. It's pretty damned simple. You don't have to buy a ton of decorations or carve a pumpkin if you don't want to, so stop whinging about "don't have time" this or "can't afford" that. Twenty

bucks worth of candy and a porch light…that's all you need.

These are the rules, so suck it up, stop being such a selfish asshole and just play along…your pathetic self-exclusion isn't impressing anyone. You want to drive on society's roads and use society's power grid to run your damn gadgets? Then you take one fucking night to give a little something for the kids in society who haven't yet turned into lazy, selfish ingrates like you. Stop being one of the formative dumps the world takes on these children who might actually have some hope in their souls.

So, with the greatest love and respect, I beg of you: Please put some effort into participating in your local Halloween next year. It doesn't have to be much effort, but it sure means a lot.

And to our readers in less-Halloween-tradition-based countries, please join in the fun! Put on some costumes, invite some friends over, watch spooky movies and have some bloody fun together! Trust me, you will enjoy yourselves. As irritating, obnoxious and disheartening as this world tends to be most of the time, any excuse to get together and celebrate with friends is a thing to cherish.

And when you get to do it in a crazy costume, it's freakin' *awesome*.

So let's do it right next year, whaddya say!

Great, now that we've got that unpleasantness outta the way, we can get to the reason we're all here: Some seriously spooktacular shenanigans! Again we've crammed together a (mostly-) horror-themed collection of weird and obscure flick-filled fun for you to enjoy while you come down from your crazy Halloween candy-induced sugar rush. Remember: 9 out of 10 physicians recommend *Weng's Chop* over a diabetic coma. (That 10th physician was a freakin' psychopath, by the way…I can't in good conscience recommend his services.) So wipe off the greasepaint, brush your teeth, inject that insulin, kick back and enjoy our Spooktacular Special! Happy Halloweenovember!

~ Tony Strauss, co-editor

NOW AVAILABLE!

50 Jack-o'-Lanterns
Heather Paxton

Art By Heather series proudly presents "The Halloween Pumpkin Digest"

Heather Paxton loves Halloween. In fact, after her birthday and Christmas, Halloween is her favorite day of the year. She enjoys drawing Jack-o'-lanterns, vampires, werewolves, Frankenstein monsters, mummies, and all sort of ghoulies and ghosties that happen to coincide with that oh so special holiday.

56 full color pages of classic Jack-o'-lanterns by Heather only $9.95 through createspace and amazon.com

CHILDHOOD REVISTED --- ALMOST

Something happened to the world of children's film fare in the 1970s. I place the blame squarely on the shoulders of post-Vietnam era peacenick parents and educational do-gooders. Maybe I am recalling a slightly different reality, but there were times when Saturday morning cartoons, afternoon Kidvid, and matinee family entertainment was full of violence and the eternal battle of good vs evil which typically accumulated in the bloody demise of "the bad guy". Somewhere around the time of The Shazam/Isis Hour of Power, *what was sometimes the best and weirdest forms of children's entertainment was slowly being eviscerated.*

That was the beginning of my article on "Fantasy Kid/Family Films in India". I sat and stared at that opening paragraph for two weeks. I sat and watched fifteen films I had planned on covering. I sat and thought a lot about what I was going to write. The article slowly began to evolve, and then I eventually began to commit ideas to the page (or in this case to a text document).

A multitude of articles could be written about all the wonderful life-altering children's television which was instrumental in the creation of the baby-boomer generation. Saturday morning cartoons prior to 1970 were full of righteous violence. Jonny Quest *is a prime example. In this 1966 American animated series, Jonny, a blond-haired teen, shoulder rifles and faces down the bad guys. People are killed. Death was a reality.* Jonny Quest *was reality-based (although it did deal with SF and horror themes), but death was also part of the superhero genre as well. A memorable episode of* The New Adventures of Superman *cartoon from 1966 was called "The Pernicious Parasite", a tale wherein a criminal discovers he has the talent to absorb energy after a dose of radiation. In the final moments of the tale he chooses to drain all of Superman's alien power, and does so with deadly results. He greedily absorbs all he can from the Krypton but O.D.s on all the power. The sequence where he is running down a roadway flanked by warehouse screaming as his body begins to expand and then explodes is one burned forever in my brain. This was before the embarrassingly touchy-feely days of* The Super Friends *(1973-1986). KidVid imports of the 1960s included* Thunderbirds *(1966, UK),* Ultraman *(ウルトラマン / Urutoraman , 1966, Japan),* Johnny Sokko and His Flying Robot *(ジャイ アントロボ / Jaianto robo, Japan, 1967),* Marine Boy *(海底少年マリン / Kaitei Shōnen Marin, Japan, 1966), and many others; the list is a long one. These were all very brutal "children's programming" written and produced for the imaginative (and often violent) minds of youth the world over. There was nothing wrong with them.*

Nothing that a kid would object to. But of course there were the "adults" and their psychiatrics that had to weigh in. Similar officials also decimated the comic industry in the 1950s.

Children's films often followed a similar vein. That is, when there were movies made for kids. A great many people consider Disney's **SNOW WHITE**, **DUMBO**, *and other such movie as children's films. However, if you ever really watched them, they are full of life and death situations. Uncensored, skewed, and prejudicial at times to be true, but many such tales, both fantastic and those based in our reality, offered thrills and chills for a hunger brain. Many of the weirdest offerings were, again, from the foreign film industry. In the 1960s and early '70s matinees were chockfull of creepy Mexican and German films based on popular fairy tales like "Puss in Boots", "Red Riding Hood" and so forth. Again, the filmatic history of Children's Entertainment will make for a huge in-depth article, but for the most part films from India have been shut out of any recent articles that I am aware. In fact the five largest producers of children cinema in the late 1950s throughout the 1970s were Germany, Japan, England, Mexico, and the United States.*

I had to stop there because it dawned on me that I was opening the preverbal "can of worms" which would then have to be dealt with. In other words, this subject was too vast for the article I had planned. It wouldn't fit into this special half issue of *Weng's Chop*. "You have *Monster!* #10 to finish and *Monster! International* #1 to complete." At least that's what I kept telling myself. "Keep it simple. There's an entire history of Children's Cinema to explore one of these days; keep on track. ONLY Indian cinema."

Man, that was a tough sell. I didn't buy it. The deadline for *Weng's Chop* #6.5 had come and gone and there was issue seven to consider. In a month I have around Fifty Indian Ghostly Possession Films to write about, and that included time for research research! Yeow!

I gave it another go:

India's own brand of children's entertainment was developed as a sub-genre, not unlike what happened with the rest of the world, albeit a bit later than most. In the early days of their cinema what usually passed for family entertainment film were Mythologicals. The fantastic variety that I will briefly review seemed to developed around the same time as many of the best (and weirdest) Taiwanese family entertainment, and that would be in the 1980s. Prior to that, films like Tapan Sinha's 1977 film **SAFED HAATHI** *("The White Elephant") were the norm, wherein children were heavily involved in the plot, which was sometimes socio-political in nature. While it is true that children are often depicted as the apple in the eye of the Indian community (with doting parents and so forth), the truth was that they weren't a viable finical incentive to Indian filmmakers. It seems that most*

5

early films that involved children were either Mythologicals about Krishna as a child, or socio-dramas like Franz Osten's **DURGA** *(1939)*. Anything really resembling family entertainment of a fantastic nature didn't come along until...

That's about as far as I got. Hit a wall cold. This article will have to wait for a future issue. I can list two of the titles I had considered covering:

KOI MILL GAYA (2003, D: Rakesh Roshan, music: Rakesh Roshan, cast: Rekha, Hrithik Roshan, Preity, Zinta, Rajat Bedi) Hindi language.This is one of the few Indian science fiction films which feature a cute little alien that kind of resembles the creature from Steven Spielberg's **E.T. THE EXTRA-TERRESTRIAL** (1982). However, before you call foul ball and start finger-pointing you should know that **KOI MILL GAYA** has its roots in an un-filmed script from the 1960s. Bengali filmmaker Satyajit Ray penned "The Alien", as it was going to be called, and based it off his 1966 short story "Bankubabur Bandhu" / "Mr. Banku's Friend". The script was shopped around, and he even had a co-production deal in the works with Columbia Pictures, but nothing happened. Rumor has it Spieberg got his mits on the script and, um, the rest is history...more or less.

Original art by director Satyajit Ray for his 1966 short story "Mr. Banku's Friend". Inspiration for Spielberg's E.T.? Probably. Did Ray get any credit? Nope.

ROBO (2008, D: Dr. R. Prasanna Kumar, Music: Nedumkunnam Sreedev. K.P. Jyothikumar, cast: Master Praveen Prasanna, Madhu, Shankar, Indrans, Kochupreman, Monilal, Sanal Kumar, Archana, Kulapulli Leela) Malayalam language. Bumbling but good-natured scientist creates a robot pal for his young son, who is later sent away to stay with an extended family. Robo shows up and they go on all sort of zany adventures together. Eventually the local religious right gets wind of the robot and decides they need to have it removed from society. Lucky for Robo, the diminutive android has a faithful following of brattish children to help it stay one step ahead of the angry elders. Low-budget hilarious hijinks to follow. Seriously, it's awful.

How's that for dangling the carrot? I'm sure you're all champing at the bit to hear more about these classics. Of course, I liked them for what they are: weird shit you don't normally see in the USA. That's what *Weng's Chop* is all about. Don't fret none, because I am still stoked to cover all of these wacky flicks, just not right now.

~ Tim Paxton, co-editor

VCD sleeve art for **ROBO**

Correction notice for Weng's Chop #6, page 131: The **BEACH BALL** pic in the middle shows Frankie Valli & The Four Seasons, *not* The Wigglers

REVIEWS

CURSE OF THE DOLL PEOPLE

(*Muñecos infernales*, a.k.a. **DEVIL DOLL MEN**)

Reviewed by Brian Harris

Forget Chucky. Don't even bother with Annabelle. If you want truly creepy doll action, diabolically driven and murderous, you're going to need to get your hands on—and watch—the Mexican horror film production, **MUÑECOS INFERNALES** (a.k.a. **THE CURSE OF THE DOLL PEOPLE**, 1961), directed by Benito Alazraki (**ESPIRITISMO** [1962], **SANTO CONTRA LOS ZOMBIES** [1962])! Some throw the word "classic" around quite a bit, basically anything B&W these days is referred to as classic, but so few B-movies actually deserve the title. I think using "vintage" in some cases instead of "classic" is apt. And after having said that, I'm going to be a total douche and insist **MUÑECOS INFERNALES** is a Mexican horror classic, right up there with **THE BLACK PIT OF DR. M** (*Misterios de ultratumba*, 1959), **BRAINIAC** (*El barón del terror*, 1962), **THE VAMPIRE** (*El vampiro*, 1957), and **THE BOOK OF STONE** (*El libro de piedra*, 1969). That's right, how do you like me now?! I tell you not to do it, then I do it! Seriously though, Mexico—like so many other countries out there—doesn't have a grand tradition of horror cinema like we here in the States, so when truly memorable films like this one come along, it's hard not to shovel on the praise. Sure, it's still a B-movie with a high cheese factor, and certainly nowhere near as good as films like **THE LIVING COFFIN** (*El grito de la muerte*, 1959) or **THE WITCH** (*La bruja*, 1954), but it's perfectly suited for a Halloween night viewing! People always want to go *balls to the wall* horror on Halloween, with all the guts, gore, torture, and dismemberment they can handle—and that's fine if that's your thing—but I'd like to recommend something creepy instead, something that makes you go, "Oh man, those are the dolls of my nightmares!"

While on a trip to Haiti, a few friends—one an unscrupulous antiquities collector—check out an "authentic" voodoo ceremony. Dissatisfied with what they felt was nothing more than a show for the tourists, they make a deal with a local to lead them to a real ritual to spy on. It's there they see a stone idol worshiped by the voodoo Houngans (Priests) as their god. Deciding to steal it, they return later and successfully make off with the artifact, but not without consequence as the men are cursed for their sacrilege. They and their families are marked for death.

When each of the men begins falling victim to odd maladies, all signs point to strange dolls featuring the likenesses of the ill-fated men. Dr. Armando Valdés (Ramón Gay, **LA MOMIA AZTECA** [1957]), his girlfriend Karina (Elvira Quintana), and gangster

Molinar (Roberto G. Rivera, **FRANKESTEIN EL VAMPIRO Y COMPAÑÍA** [1962]) join together to track down the Houngan (Quintín Bulnes, **TOM THUMB AND LITTLE RED RIDING HOOD** [1962]) responsible for the horror before they end up his victims as well.

Written by Alfredo Salazar (**HERENCIA DIABÓLICA** [1994]), and adapted from Abraham Merritt's 1932 tale *Burn, Witch, Burn!*, which was originally serialized in pulp fiction magazine *Argosy Weekly*, **MUÑECOS INFERNALES** is a pretty straightforward tale of supernatural revenge. Mess with the forces of darkness and you'll get burned. This film is overflowing with morality! Most of the characters waste what little breath they have scoffing at the possibility of paranormal retribution and dismissing good Catholic—well versed in anthropology and the dark arts—Karina. Naturally this makes each demise all the more delicious as they pay for their sin with their lives. What we're left with is Karina, her dedicated boyfriend Armando and skeptical crime boss Molinar, all tasked with fighting evil the only way they know how. Unfortunately Molinar and his thugs find their guns useless when dealing in the realm of the spiritual. Don't hate, even a criminal can be a saint when the cause is righteous! While the murderous little dolls—filled with the souls of the dead men—are evil, they can also be seen as agents of the Lord, sent to punish one another for their mutual disbelief. And what of poor Staloon, the voodoo zombie resurrected to serve the forces of evil? One can only surmise that his zombification was penance for also being a damnable sinner before he died, like the dolls.

Dubbed for American television, **MUÑECOS INFERNALES** was released stateside as **CURSE OF THE DOLL PEOPLE**, trimmed of 13 minutes. Why cut this film when it so effectively illustrates the misfortunes that may befall those that mock powers from beyond? Not really sure but noticeably missing from the U.S. cut is the murder of a nurse and the accompanying black magic ceremony performed by the Houngan to transfer her soul from dying body to awaiting doll. Did they cut it to remove the black magic? Or the nurse and her doll counterpart—which never shows up again in the film? Or was it the human heart sliced open, its interior blood poured on the doll? I'm going to go with all of the above.

What is it about **MUÑECOS INFERNALES** that freaks me out so much? I'll tell you: the dolls. These aren't your average dolls, they're perfectly formed little people (read: *midgets!*) wearing *stunning* masks that look remarkably like the victims they're meant to represent! I just couldn't believe this film was made in '60/'61 with such detailed, well-crafted masks. They literally looked like smaller versions of the actors, and

The top three pics show eerie scenes from **MUÑECOS INFERNALES. Above:** Elvira Quintana, heroine of the same film, combats evil the tried-and-trusted RC way.

Quintín Bulnes as the evil voodoo *houngan*, with one of his "little people"

that kicked this film up a few notches for me. Oh, and did I mention their weapon of choice? *Ice picks*. Dolls with ice picks, that's really creepy shit. The acting and sets were all great, the voodoo priest was adequately groovy and evil at the same time, and Staloon the zombie was gross and kick-ass, but the dolls make this film and their antics throughout will keep you riveted to this B-movie gem, wondering just what in hell you'll see next.

Here's the kicker though, the Mexican version of **MUÑECOS INFERNALES** isn't currently available on DVD with English subtitles. Why VCI didn't go the extra mile and simply download the English subtitles from the Internet and add them to the DVD is anybody's guess, but they do offer the sliced 'n' diced English-language version of the film as an extra. My suggestion: purchase the DVD, rip the uncut version to your computer, download the English subtitles yourself and watch 'til your heart is content. I cannot recommend this film enough to those of you seeking something unique, strange, creepy and fun.

1961, MEXICO. D: BENITO ALAZRAKI / PAUL NAGLE (DUBBING DIRECTOR)
AVAILABLE FROM VCI ENTERTAINMENT

THE DEVIL
(邪魔 / *Xie mo*, a.k.a. **DEVIL'S EXPRESS**)

Reviewed by Eric Messina

A girl in a scarf gets her head bashed in with a rock during the credits. Then, in a Shaw Brothers-type voodoo hut, a man is split open like a dressed hog, as a witch played by Lau Yin-Sueng (a.k.a. Liu Yin-Shang), roots around in his entrails and spices them up with some Lawry's seasoned salt. His guts are infested with maggots and other assorted critters.

This movie doesn't give you a moment to breathe as the traumatic snake-puking gore is doled out in heaping bucketfuls. The sorceress warns the man—who should definitely be dead—that he must stay away from drinking and girls. I doubt he listens, in this cautionary tale of witchcraft, domestic abuse, rash decisions and Screamin' Jay Hawkins-type mumbo jumbo. The dubbing is prime *Godzilla* style (high pitched and whiny or sluggishly paced).

Mr. Chao checks into a hotel where the children are bellhops. One kid, whose name is Ding Dong (played by Au Dai, a.k.a. Ou Di), wears the same outfit as Timothy the mouse, who guided Dumbo throughout all his adventures.

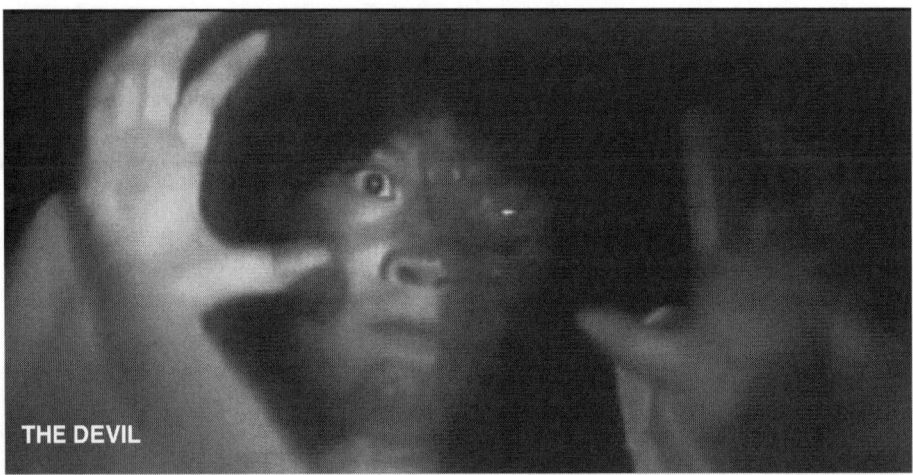

THE DEVIL

These Asian characters say Western Slang like "I'll fix you" or British slang like "You're a cheeky little bugger". During a bar scene, they actually play "The Stranger" by Billy Joel! I doubt the "Piano Man" is aware of this clever bit of copyright infringement and they loosely cover it up in Muzak fashion with flutes and string instruments. It's an odd choice, over the usual stolen Goblin music associated with other Asian filmmakers. Tsui Hark early in his career used a few Simonetti copyrighted tracks for **WE'RE GOING TO EAT YOU** (地獄無門 / *Di yu wu men*, 1980) and **DANGEROUS ENCOUNTERS OF THE FIRST KIND** (第一類型危險 *Di yi lei xing wei sian*, 1980). I'm always pleasantly surprised at what bits of Western pop culture are used throughout different Hong Kong films. **7 LUCKY NINJA KIDS** (a 1989-released US reedit of the 1986 HK film **LUCKY SEVEN** [7小福 / *7 xiao fu*]) might set a world's record for stolen copyrighted themes from other films like **HALLOWEEN** (1978), **CAT PEOPLE** (1982) and **ROCKY** (1976).

In this film, a floating witch with a gruesome oversized eyeball and melted face scares the shit out of a man in the forest. It not only freaks him out, but causes him to explode into hideous green and red boils (just in time for Christmas!); he also upchucks snakes. My theory is that an *onryō*, the same vengeful female ghost seen in **YOTSUYA KAIDAN** (四谷怪談 a.k.a. **ILLUSION OF BLOOD**, 1965), is responsible.

Ding Dong the bellhop loves money and helps Mr. Koo (or Chao, played by Sherman Chow Shiu-Dung, a.k.a. Chou Shao Tung) find himself a girlfriend. The hotel manager slaps him in the head a lot and it's a bit uncomfortable. Maybe they are an Asian slapstick comedy team, I'm unaware of—who knows? The kid doesn't even seem to have a home and sleeps in the lobby of the hotel at the desk like the clerks in **MYSTERY TRAIN** (1989), the film by Jim Jarmusch! No child labor laws are present in **THE DEVIL**, which is part of its evil nature.

The grisly female specter uses snakes as a weapon, and likes to drop them on your crotch while you're sleeping; pretty damn scary if you ask me! This film is on some kind of warped speed, because as fast as the dribbling pus scenes assault your senses, Mr. Chao's relationship turns immediately into marriage. I mean, had they put up a "years later" slate signaling a time lapse, it might've been less abrupt.

Before you can say "honeymoon", the ghost from the dark forest returns and scares Chao—luckily she doesn't cause *him* to mutate into a puddle of bile and creepy crawlies.

I felt sorry for one nameless poor sap the ghost virus infects, who was just unlucky enough to stumble by the cursed hotel. He is callously wrangled up by the workers and burnt alive! I guess they want to stave off the ghost-vomit plague, but that was just cruel. Everything about this scene is ghastly and it abruptly cuts

The Devils

off as a sympathetic, teary-eyed Ding Dong looks on. What the fuck is going on here? There's never an explanation as to why the crowd has turned into a lynch mob and it's pretty disturbing.

Domestic abuse starts to rear its ugly face between Shirley (Wong Bo-Yuk, a.k.a. Wang Bao Yu) and Chao; it may be the result of ghostly possession or the fact that they rushed head-first into marriage without properly getting to know each other first!

Chao becomes a total dick and pisses everyone off; he's an idiot, who apparently has a black magic wizard relative who could have helped him, but instead he blows his chances by stabbing the guy. After the hotel manager—also known as Ding Dong's comedy counterpart—is killed, that's the last straw for the witch. They devise a plan to kill Chao with sorcery. Whenever the witch talks, she sounds like Mata Hairy from *Lancelot Link: Secret Chimp* on Quaaludes.

THE DEVIL is a lot of fun for Asian horror fans of knock-off chop-socky dubbing and Shaw Bros-type antics. Some of the revolting multicolored body explosions reminded me of **STREET TRASH** (1987), if it were lit by a flashlight. This film is oddly compelling, even with all its flaws and inconsistencies.

If you're scratching your head and wondering about where the devil or devils in this film are, don't hold your

breath because there are none at all. If it wasn't for Chas Balun's VHS bootleg catalog I would've never heard of this movie, which he describes as "stupid as shit with an alarmingly high slime-o-rama gross out quotient". I also have to give Jack Jensen credit, whose 'blog *Backyard-Asia.blogspot.com* always guides me in the right direction in finding impossibly rare films from the mysterious and treacherous Orient. For anyone looking for a copy, Videoasia's *Tales of Voodoo Volume 3* offers a cheapie transfer under the title **DEVIL'S EXPRESS**. Apprehensive Films also released the film on DVD, but according to some of the bad reviews knocking their bare-bones VHS transfer, it sounds like **THE DEVIL** shall remain in all its dingy glory on a hard-to-find crummy videotape format.

1981, HONG KONG. D: REN-CHIEH CHANG
AVAILABLE FROM APPREHENSIVE FILMS
AND VIDEOASIA

RED TEARS: SWORD OF BLOOD

(紅涙 / レッド・ティアーズ, a.k.a. **RED TEARS – KÔRUI**, a.k.a. **MONSTER KILLER**)

Reviewed by Brian Harris

Remember when zombie films (horror) were sort of swallowed up by the pandemic/outbreak films (medical thrillers), and for awhile there it was difficult to decide whether you were witnessing infected people driven beyond sanity or the living dead? It all blurred together, combining elements from both into what seemed to be something not entirely zombie and not entirely pandemic/outbreak, no doubt fueling many an epic Internet flame war. Neo-zombists have welcomed in the infected, just as Romero's ghouls were eventually welcomed in by those who felt zombies could only be created by means of voodoo. Zombies can now run (**DAWN OF THE DEAD** [2004]), think and speak (**RETURN OF THE LIVING DEAD** [1985]), use weapons (**DAY OF THE DEAD** [1985]) and even fall in love (**WARM BODIES** [2013])! *The blasphemy!*

Zombies aren't the only monsters changing. Vampires have also been merging with the medical thriller as time has gone on, focusing on blood-borne viral strains and parasitic infections while slowly ushering out the supernatural elements. That's nothing new to horror fans, of course, as there have been several well-received films that have presented vampirism as an illness or disease, such as **NEAR DARK** (1987), **DAYBREAKERS** (2009) and **BLADE** (1998). Unfortunately, the "infected" angle has pushed the reluctant vampire to the forefront, presenting them as unwilling victims torn between their humanity and the disease that drives them to take the lives of their fellow man for sustenance. They seek a cure and forgiveness for the acts they committed while afflicted. Instead of immortal whiners, we get sick ones. It's not always an unwelcome concept really, and these days the reluctant vampire is widely accepted, but there's still a place for the blood-thirsty, shape-shifting, supernatural predator.

Enter **RED TEARS** (2011), one of the many overseas horror films that received a U.S. release with nary a word from fans before slipping into obscurity. Not Pinoy action/crime film obscurity or anything; more like, "Who released this and when?" obscurity. The who and when is simple: Xenon—yeah they're still around—back in February of '13, right around the ass-end of the Japanese splatter wave. Nowhere near as bloody or freaky as **TOKYO GORE POLICE** (東京残酷警察 / *Tôkyô zankoku keisatsu*, 2008]), cute or gory as **VAMPIRE GIRL VS. FRANKENSTEIN GIRL** (吸血少女対少女フランケン / *Kyûketsu Shôjo tai Shôjo Furanken*, 2009) or as nutty as **ROBOGEISHA** (ロボゲイシャ, 2009), Takanori Tsujimoto, director of **HARD REVENGE, MILLY: BLOODY BATTLE** (ハード・リベンジミリー ブラッディバトル / *Hâdo ribenji, Mirî: Buraddi batoru*, 2009), still delivered on many of the elements fans of Asian horror and action films have come to expect. If you're a fan of Japanese Tokusatsu and gritty HK action-crime, and forgiving of low budgets, I think **RED TEARS** may hit the spot.

A rash of gruesome beheadings have the police working overtime to find a culprit, and green detective Tetsuo Nojima (Yuma Ishigaki of **13 ASSASSINS** [十

三人の刺客 / *Jûsan-nin no shikaku*, 2010]) thinks he may have found a possible lead. Instead of a crazed killer though, he meets a beautiful young woman named Sayoko (Natsuki Kato, **STACY** [2001]), whom he becomes enamored with. Meanwhile, grizzled veteran detective Mishima (Yasuaki Kurata, **BRUCE LEE AND I** [李小龍與我 / *Qi lin zhang*, 1973]) believes there's more to Sayoko and her invalid mother (Karin Yamaguchi) than meets the eye, and he's determined to flush out their true nature.

Watching **RED TEARS** I was initially struck by its similarity in tone to Jôji Iida's **ANOTHER HEAVEN** [アナザーヘブン / *Anaza hevun*, 2000]), a low-budget supernatural police procedural thriller released to little reception back in 2003 under the Fangoria Films DVD imprint. Both have a similar setup as well, but **RED TEARS** has three things **ANOTHER HEAVEN** didn't: a full-on man-in-a-monster-suit battle; the ultra-cool, ultra bad-ass Yasuaki Kurata; and wire work à la HK action films!

Though Kurata plays a police officer in this film, he holds himself like an old school yakuza: head down, confident, coiled like a deadly viper prepared to lash out any second with extreme violence. His character is hard not to love, which makes sense as the film was essentially written for him by director Takanori Tsujimoto and co-writer Yonekawa Eiichi. Not only is his character as cool as a cucumber, but Kurata-san does his own stunts—the guy runs an action/stunt school in Japan! The wire work wasn't as outrageous as it could have been—they went the action route instead of fantasy—but it still spiced-up what could have been a ho-hum affair to due to budgetary constraints. It's also interesting to note that it was Kurata's Kurata Promotion Company that first introduced wire work to Japanese cinema back in 2003 with the film **YELLOW DRAGON** (*Kôryû: Ierô doragon*).[1]

Remember when I mentioned this wasn't as blah-blah-blah as **TOKYO GORE POLICE, VAMPIRE GIRL VS. FRANKENSTEIN GIRL** or **ROBO-GEISHA**? Well, I stand by that. However, this film does share something in common with all three of those films, and that would be the presence of special makeup effects whiz kid and filmmaker Yoshihiro Nishimura; it's no wonder the creature and gore sequences were so familiar and fun. Thankfully they didn't throw either at viewers every chance they got, instead opting to give you small doses here and there until the final quarter of the film, when the action really heats up. When it's time for the grue and blood geysers, we get 'em!

Quick aside: I thought the title's connection to the visual appearance of the vampires in this film was pretty damn clever.

RED TEARS is entertaining, the characters are engaging, the effects work was effective and the action was impressive; it's no **RIGOR MORTIS** (殭屍 / *Geung si*, 2013]), but it still deserves to be seen by those Asian horror cinema fans eager to check out some small-scale thrills. It's a shame Xenon went with a DVD cover design that feels more at home with a yakuza film than horror; I can see horror fans passing right by this production, assuming it's crime or action. If you see it, check it out. For a few bucks less than $10, I'd consider owning it.

2011, JAPAN. D: TAKANORI TSUJIMOTO
AVAILABLE FROM XENON PICTURES

1 Brasor, Philip (October 29, 2011). "Japanese Eyes 'Monster Killer'". *Tokyo International Film Festival.* http://2011.tiff-jp.net/news/en/?p=1188

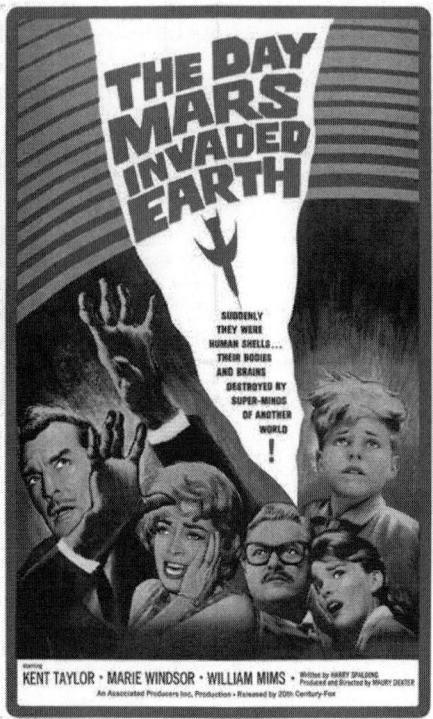

THE DAY MARS INVADED EARTH

Reviewed by Steve Fenton

"Is there life on Mars?" is the big question heard asked here. And the answer is yes, but it isn't living on Mars, it's down here with us…*again!*

Having been launched into outer space on an Atlas rocket, the Mariner B spacecraft deposits a landing module on the Red Planet. Dispatched to explore that new world by means of a state-of-the-art robotic device, said automated, free-roving device is there destroyed by an unknown force, which reduces it to smoldering wreckage. While only of brief duration, this introductory sequence is rendered rather well, all things considered: utilizing a metallic mechanical model trundling wonkily over a Chesley Bonestell-esque miniature Martian landscape. While obviously done on a tiny scale with minuscule resources, the sequence shows that at least some creative effort was expended to get the job done. This promising intro leads into a plot in which—as per our advance expectations of the title—Mars gets its own back by launching a retaliatory strike against our Earth (although their claim is, "We're not here out of vindictiveness"). If all this sounds potentially spectacular, don't get your hopes up…it *isn't*. But points for trying. Although of only 70 minutes in duration, the runtime largely crawls by like three hours spent watching paint dry (or perhaps a whole week's worth of *Corrie Street*!).

During the Christmas season, Dr. David Fielding (Kent Taylor [1907-1987]) and his immediate family "camp out" at the palatial Florida estate owned by relatives of his wife Claire Fielding (Marie Windsor [1919-2000], star of **CAT-WOMEN OF THE MOON** [1953, USA], who, having played some memorably fiery vixens in her time herein mostly plays it like a blandly servile upper middle class American housewife, more's the pity; and not only that, but at times here she vaguely evokes comedienne Carol Burnett, of all people!). After the couple—along with their preteen son Rocky (Gregg Shank) and adolescent daughter Judy (Betty Beall)—find themselves inescapably trapped on the grounds of the mansion due to its electrically powered front gate malfunctioning—thanks to an act of sabotage by forces unknown— and becoming locked, the nuclear family faces harassment by an otherworldly power beyond their comprehension (and ours too, at times; possibly even the scripter's as well). At one point upon hearing eerie electronic tonalities—evidently piped in from Mars—through the earpiece of a telephone, Ms. Windsor says in a haunted tone, "It's *unearthly*". Elsewhere, half-hearted allusions are made that perhaps the old dark house serving as the family unit's temporary home away from home may be suffering from a haunting by ghostly apparitions…which we of course already learned well in advance are actually of extraterrestrial rather than supernatural origin.

Essentially what we have here is yet another variation—derived from a mostly fairly literate script by **THE EARTH DIES SCREAMING** (1964) and **CURSE OF THE FLY**'s (1965) screenwriter Harry Spalding (1913-2008)—of the old and oft-used **INVASION OF THE BODY SNATCHERS** (1956) "human duplicates" idea (three years later in '65, Hugo Grimaldi's and Arthur C. Pierce's **THE HUMAN DUPLICATORS** reutilized some rudimentarily similar themes, if presenting them in a far more luridly ludicrous manner, in full-color rather than B&W…and with the recently late Richard Kiel as a towering humanoid alien too, no less!). Unlike **BODY SNATCHERS**, in our present title, rather than springing full-grown from giant seed-pods into corporeal beings, these insidious "passive-aggressive" invaders have no physical brain or body, consisting of nothing but energy; a concept which hadn't been as done to death by the early-'60s as it has been by now (it seems as if every single sci-fi series made since the original *Outer Limits* has had at least one episode involving some kind of energy being). Because energy can neither be created nor destroyed, only changed into different forms, in the present film these bodiless and brainless (if by no means mindless) beings—described by one of their kind as "manifestations of intelligence"—are free to drift around and assume new physical bodies at will, where needed. Rather than this procedure being presented via elaborate special effects, people's faces merely momentarily go all blurry when they are subjected to the alien influence and their "duplication" occurs, whereupon the picture abruptly comes back into focus again to indicate that the transmutation is complete. Because the "lookalike" versions don't automatically cancel-out their originals, this means that both the superficially exact copy and the original are simultaneously extant on the same plane of existence, due to which—needless to say—various predictable complications arise. In one scene, Windsor is "pursued" by the footsteps of her husband's doppelgänger; only to run smack-dab into the arms of her real one. Due to the fact that the couple is going through a period of marital conflict, this duplicity of their characters was presumably intended as some sort of symbolic touch. The script also seems to be striving to make some pointed commentary on conjugal/familial alienation. Elsewhere, the couple's daughter Judy encounters "herself" in the interests of further murky messaging. However, whatever potential symbolism may be lurking here somewhere in the nebulous shadowy recesses hardly seems worth taking the trouble of digging out in this resolutely unexciting if by no means totally pathetic context.

To make it easier on the special effects department—not that, considering the general dearth of FX, they had it too rough on this shoot—Miss Beall's "alienated" twin was played by her real-life identical twin sister, Barbara. Hence, no complicated composite shots or specially made-up doubles were required for the scene wherein the real deal encounters the phony-baloney version of herself and, in a display of "sibling rivalry", the pair engage in a brief and decidedly restrained catfight at close quarters; action which would be a cinch to fabricate in this the digital age using CG, but was vastly more difficult to accomplish convincingly (if at all) back in the days when practical and optical effects were about the only ways to go, and anything too elaborate was well out of the price range of modest-budgeted movies like this one. Potential farcical situations involving the interaction of the original versions and their alien doubles are never realized, possibly for the better. Although, then again, perhaps some intentional humor might have helped, but such is this film's uniformity of blandness that there's barely even any *un*intentional yuks to be had, which can often be the saving grace of low-grade thrillers like this.

Seeing double so to speak, in what amounts to one of the movie's strongest scenes, star Taylor—an underrated actor commonly associated with "bad" SF B-flicks (who, it should be said gives an assured, nuanced and compelling dual performance here, for the most part)—is confronted by his outwardly identical imitation (i.e., a business-suited body double with similar fashion sense if not actual duplicate cloth-ing, mostly seen from the rear in "over-the-shoulder" shots crosscutting back and forth between the "two" Taylors, acting off each other), who explains the source of the mysterious events. It seems that some sort of Martian intelligence was accidentally beamed to our world during a power surge from the malfunctioning Mars lander robot; which might well amount to an interesting idea in a better film, but here it's just…well, kinda *meh*. Now down here among us, in an interesting twist—even if it does rather expose the title as a bit of a cheat—the Martians are allegedly not intent on invading *our* world, but are merely trying to prevent us from invading *theirs*. ("An invasion?" asks Taylor of "himself". "Oh, not at all", replies the dead-spit of him. "*You* invaded *us*. All we wish to do is protect ourselves… When the time comes, we'll try to be what your people call 'humane.'") This longish dialogue exchange between the "two" Taylors incorporates one rather well-done composite shot of the actor in "double vision" as he meets "himself" face to face. However, in the unletterboxed TV print of the film I watched, most of the Taylor on the left-hand side of the screen (i.e., his alien version) was cropped off, spoiling what would otherwise be a quite decent if simple effect.

For the climax, Taylor's onscreen scientist colleague Webb, co-star William Mims' character—whose eyeglasses have lenses the size of portable TV screens!—after jimmying open the seized main gate in a frantic getaway attempt, has a fateful showdown with the entire duplicate Fielding family, and is ultimately reduced to nothing more than a flaming man-shaped outline of ashes on the bottom of the mansion's waterless in-ground swimming pool. The most visually inventive and shocking image—unfortunately a textbook case of too little, too late—is the final one, but at least it's *something* we can hang onto. And the twist is: the Martians win. (*Oops!* Guess I gave the game away.) All I can say is, if only the rest of the film (or even just a few more parts of it interspersed throughout the narrative) had displayed such inventiveness as we see just before the final fade, then **THE DAY MARS INVADED EARTH** might have turned out a whole lot more special than it did(n't).

So, on a more positive note, because I'm loath to give this well-meaning film a total trashing, I should perhaps mention that performances by the small cast are naturalistic and highly competent, but, back on the downside again, the dramatic interaction between players for the most part results in a distinct lack of either tension or atmosphere (such as in the "two" Taylors' much too civil and strictly verbal confrontation). Complete with weepy strings, Richard LaSalle's score lists to the overly sentimental side. Lacking any bug-eyed monsters and even short on SFX other than for those out-of-focus "alien" facials, what we're left with is an interesting concept severely compromised by resoundingly mediocre execution. It's not all-out

A Toltec demon from **THE DARK POWER**

bad by any means, it's just too bland for its own good, and its small-scale, less than spectacular structure—wholly bereft of any scenes of mass-destruction caused by flying saucer attacks or other grander-scale action, as its grandiose title might seem to imply—hardly warranted the CinemaScope format for its presentation, as the comparatively restrictive confines of a smaller screen might have better supported its theme by endowing a more oppressively claustrophobic mood (in fact, other than for its window-boxed opening titles, the televised print I saw was presented fullscreen, as is the upload available for viewing on YouTube, which was ripped from a VHS taping of a TV airing on the Fox Movie Channel, whose watermark is periodically seen onscreen throughout). And speaking of television, when I first saw this movie aired on Canada's SPACE station back at the tail end of the '90s, it—presumably on basis of its title—was specifically intended to flog Mars bars during endless commercial breaks which only made the running time seem that much more protractedly interminable and unendurable. That said, I watched it again recently, this time without commercials, to see if that might improve the pacing any. And I decided it definitely does. I'm all for giving movies a second chance, especially ones of this more misbegotten, lesser-seen sort, which I'm hesitant to be too harsh on, simply because it had the deck stacked against it right from its inception due to its lowly origins and even lower budget, and I'm a real one for supporting the underdog where I can, me. That's just the way I'm made (as Popeye might say, "I yam what I yam").

To sum up: They say that a watched pot never boils. With a nifty title like this one's got, you'd think it might at least have reached boiling point, even if it didn't actually boil-over. But if you're expecting a good old-fashioned schlocky sci-fi potboiler, look elsewhere, because **THE DAY MARS INVADED EARTH** barely even gets lukewarm, let alone generates any actual heat…at least, not until its dynamite final reveal, which is impressive more for stylistic reasons rather than any earth-shattering revelation of plot. Although, for those in line for some talky, static post-'50s SF whose aspirations fail to transcend its limitations, this just might fit the bill. You could definitely do a whole lot worse.

1962, USA. D: MAURY DEXTER
AVAILABLE FROM SINISTER CINEMA [OOP]

The Death of a Toltec

THE DARK POWER

Reviewed by Brian Harris

Wedged in between Lloyd Kaufman's 1984 brain-busting low-budget masterpiece **THE TOXIC AVENGER** and the bafflingly popular **NEON MANIACS** (1986) lies a little-seen creature feature that's pleasantly gory, not-at-all scary and has the unique distinction of being legendary Western cinema actor Lash LaRue's only horror film. That's right, the whip is back! Now, you young people born in the '90s will no doubt draw a blank on Lash, understandably, as Western cinema was nearly extinct by your time—outside of maybe a hundred or so films during that decade—it pretty much went the way of noir. The plotlines and conventions of the American Western may never die or be forgotten, but the actors did and have. Sadly, names like Gene Autry, Roy Rogers, Dale Evans, Tom Mix, Tex Ritter, Lash LaRue and "Gabby" Hayes are spoken of very little outside of academic and Western aficionado circles. When I read that Lash was in this film, I knew I had to own.

After a small-town Indian chief dies alone in his home, as an outcast and social pariah, his place is fixed up and prepared for rental. Despite the property's infamous reputation as land cursed by evil Toltec wizards, a group of young college women move in and make themselves at home. Naturally, when it comes time for the Indian chief to perform the required ceremony designed to keep the Toltec wizards from crossing over into our realm, he is no longer alive to do so. Now the Toltecs have rejoined the land of the living and their goal is to shed blood to feed their powerful magic. The only thing standing between the Toltecs and eternal darkness is Ranger Gerard and the sting of his deadly accurate whip! No man, woman, or undead Mesoamerican necromancer is safe from true justice!

Apparently director Phil Smoot created both this film and the low-budget sci-fi film **ALIEN OUTLAW** (1985) as vehicles for Lash and his wonder whip, which I gotta say is pretty damn cool. From Westerns and comic books to horror and sci-fi. As novel as it is though, nobody will be lining up to see this film based on Lash's presence alone, which is where the Toltec zombies come in. As I mentioned in the first paragraph, this film was released between **THE TOXIC AVENGER** and **NEON MANIACS** and the reason I bring these two films up is they all share slightly similar monsters. The creatures in **THE DARK POWER** (1985) not only look similar but sound similar as well. I had to check the credits of the FX crew for this film to make certain they had no connections to the other two films. While not in the slightest bit scary, the creatures are impressive to behold, each having its own distinct style and personality. I won't lie to you folks, I was a bit let down at first as the Toltec wizards, presented to us as bloodthirsty monsters,

Another monstrous Toltec demon from **THE DARK POWER**

be-bopped about mugging for the camera, coming off goofy and stooge-like. But as I got into the film and enjoyed the occasional explosion of gore, it didn't seem to matter as much. The real fun begins though when Lash LaRue arrives on the scene to do battle with them, carrying nothing more than his whip and a few mind-blowingly manly one-liners such as, "Feel my whip, you sonnuvabitch!" and "I wonder how you'd look without a nose?" Classic. And yes, he does whip a creature's nose off.

The acting was exactly what you would expect in a film with such a noticeably low budget; it ranged from bad to just okay. The best of the lot, by far, was the more experienced LaRue. On the story front, things take way too long to heat up, the dialogue was clunky, characters are introduced, given time to become likable only to disappear, and there even seems to be a moral to the whole affair, as evidenced by all of the drunks, racists, and promiscuous characters meeting ghastly ends. In other words, it was a B-movie through and through. Going into this film expecting big things is definitely a mistake but there's no doubt it's entertaining. If you're able to make it to the major showdown—which takes place in front of a central air unit—without bailing, you're a dyed-in-the-wool B-movie junkie.

I honestly can see why **THE DARK POWER** was sought after on VHS by tape collectors; it's an enjoyable little ride and definitely something of a cult gem. This one needs to be seen as a double-feature with Smoot's **ALIEN OUTLAW**.

By the way, if you're a all about transfers and special features, the case claims this was a new widescreen transfer taken from an interpositive that was made from the original camera negative. *But what does it all mean, Basil?* Honestly, not much to me, though I am informed enough to notice and mention the mad crazy amount of interlacing I saw throughout this film. The soundtrack was mastered from the original three stripe master, and the release features a commentary with Phil Smoot (writer/director) and Sherwood Jones (editor) and a "Remembering Lash LaRue" featurette.

1985, USA. D: PHIL SMOOT
AVAILABLE FROM VCI ENTERTAINMENT

WEREWOLF RISING

Reviewed by Brian Harris

Fans of Fangoria Magazine's **BLOOD DRIVE** short film compilations (2004 and 2005) may remember the name BC Furtney; no doubt they'll remember his short films (**MR. ERYAMS** and **DISPOSER** [both 2004]), both well made, reasonably acted, disturbing productions. As with many of the directors from the **BLOOD DRIVE** series, Furtney forged ahead to continue paying dues and feeding the ravenous beast we call life. In 2013, Image Entertainment released his first feature film **DO NOT DISTURB** (2013)—which appears to be a re-worked version of an earlier attempt entitled **NEW TERMINAL HOTEL** (2010)—to lukewarm reception. His sophomore effort **WEREWOLF RISING** appears to be receiving a bit more positive attention from online reviews, which is always nice to see when you're constantly struggling to bring creative endeavors to life.

Emma (Melissa Carnell, **HUMANS VERSUS ZOMBIES** [2011]), a beautiful young woman recovering from a tough bout with alcoholism, decides to head back to her childhood home to find solace, as well as escape from some troubling nightmares she's been experiencing. Instead of inner peace, she discovers family friend Wayne (Brian Berry, **SPLATTER BEACH** [2007]) wrestling with his own shortcomings, and convict on the loose, Johnny Lee (Matt Copko), camped out in the forest. Against her better judgment, she finds herself taking a liking to Johnny Lee and makes dinner plans with him. That night, she's not only confronted by Wayne and his drunken advances, but also discovers Johnny Lee on death's door after being attacked by a wolf!

Nothing is what it seems to be, secrets, lies and transformations emerge as Johnny Lee takes a turn for the better, Wayne continues spiraling, and an unwelcome visitor (Bill Oberst Jr., **CIRCUS OF THE DEAD** [2014]) lies in wait within the darkness of the woods, biding his time and stalking his prey.

WEREWOLF RISING is an interesting low-budget film with its fair share of problems; like the majority of independent productions with limited budgets, there are things that must be sacrificed in order for that vision to come to fruition. Most of the time, acting is where these films really take the biggest hit, as more experienced actors, naturally, cost more money. Trying to balance a competent cast with the FX needed for a film to look good—especially when it's a creature feature—can be a real pain in the ass. When watching an indie film, one simply has to be forgiving when one,

Girl To...*Grrrl!* Woman becomes wolfen in **WEREWOLF RISING.**

the other, or both come up a bit lacking. Waiting for the ax to drop, right? Well, it that won't be happening.

Furtney's film certainly had some problems; I found Emma's introductory monologue to be way too heavy on exposition, there's a sequence in which Emma escapes to Wayne's home and just so happens to discover a bottle of booze in the bottom of the closet in which she hides—a sequence that reminds me of that forehead-slapping moment when somebody finds car keys in a sun visor—and finally a completely unnecessary scene involving a young woman by a fireside that seemed to serve only to show off some tits and get in a nice kill. Don't get me wrong, I love me a fantastic rack and some gore—I'm an exploitation film fan, after all—but it came off forced and inorganic to the story. I could probably also mention continuity issues like wounds swapping sides and people appearing perfectly sober after drinking comatose-inducing amounts of alcohol, but harping on those things is just silly. No film is going to be perfect.

On the positive side, Furtney has a nice little cast here. Melissa Carnell (Emma) is a ray of onscreen sunshine. When she smiled, I found myself smiling as well. Her character felt genuine, like you were seeing Carnell and not her character. While some might consider Emma's alcoholism to be nothing more than a cheap attempt at providing her character with depth, I feel it worked here. The director intended to draw a comparison between lycanthropy and alcoholism, some may argue not well but it's there and he did.

Matt Copko (as Johnny Lee) took some getting used to at first; his acting style is a bit rough and his character was hard to like, but he grew on me as the film unfolded. It was closing in on the final act when I realized why I liked Copko so much. No joke, he reminded me of a young Nicholas Cage. Scoff all you like but I dig Cage, for the most part, even when he's doing crap. He's got this "I'm just like you" vibe that's hard to hate. Copko's got it as well. More power to him.

What can I say about Bill Oberst Jr., he's a diamond in the rough when it comes to independent cinema because the man can act his ass off. He has a look, he has range and he's got a mean work ethic—just look at his schedule for the remainder of 2014 and into 2015! The first time I saw him, which was in **NUDE NUNS WITH BIG GUNS** (2010), he left quite the impression. I then had the pleasure of talking to him on the radio a few years back about his work on **ABRAHAM LINCOLN VS. ZOMBIES** (2012), a film I genuinely enjoyed, and he proved himself to be a really well-humored, humble guy, even after I rudely compared him to actor Jürgen Prochnow. His work in this film was exceptional and it's always a pleasure to see him.

The question on everybody's mind is, "*What about the damn werewolf?!*" and I'm happy to say there

is a werewolf, it was done practically and it looked great. Furtney trips over an awkward transformation sequence, honestly it's doubtful anybody will ever measure up to **AN AMERICAN WEREWOLF IN LONDON**'s (1981) transformation, but he quickly regains his footing when we get the werewolf doing what werewolves do best. I was hoping we'd get a frenzied werewolf battle—you'll understand when you see the film—but no such luck. Still, the werewolf looked great. As a creature feature fan I appreciate a filmmaker's decision to steer clear of cheaper, though less effective, CG. It served this film well.

WEREWOLF RISING is watchable and it entertained me, and that's what it's all about. Like I always say, entertainment is king. Give it a shot…if it works for you, then it's time well spent. If not, there's always the next film!

2014, USA. D: BC FURTNEY
AVAILABLE FROM IMAGE ENTERTAINMENT

GHOST EYES
(眼鬼 / *Gui yan*)

Reviewed by Eric Messina

I was starting to worry that I'd finally hit rock bottom. You see, I'd tried some highly recommended Shaw Brothers titles recently but they hardly even eased the shakes. I need the high that I got from favorites like **SEEDING OF A GHOST** (种鬼 / *Zhong gui*, a.k.a. **BLACK MAGIC 5**, 1983), the *Black Magic* (降頭 /

Jiang tou) series, or **THE BOXER'S OMEN** (魔 / *Mo*, 1983). Once you experience that level of slapstick gruesomeness flowing through your system, you crave more, more, more of the same and you don't care if it's frying your brain like an egg because it's just…so…gooood!

The curse of the Asian exploitation-film critic is to compare everything else to those epic pinnacles of maggot-bursting, vomit-inducing, ghostly terror. You'll do anything to get that first-time feeling again. You get weary and cynical as your tolerance grows, thinking you may never get the same bizarre unhealthy satisfaction you need, like cinematic heroin. I've got a serious hankering for insanity and the only dealer who has the ability to feed my addiction right is Kuei Chih-Hung.

This brilliant filmmaker has made some of the best movies in the Shaw Bros. catalog. He's responsible for **THE KILLER SNAKES** (蛇殺手 / *She sha shou*, 1975), **VIRGINS OF THE SEVEN SEAS** (洋妓 / *Yang chi*, a.k.a. **THE BOD SQUAD**, 1974), **HEX** (邪 / *Xie*, 1980) and **THE BOXER'S OMEN**. Every one of those titles is a must-see gore-fest, loaded with face-ripping images that force bile into your throat and threaten to cause projectile vomiting, and all are incredibly directed by the same person! Director Chih-Hung is an accomplished craftsman and has created some of my favorite ghastly images from any '70s cinema, period. Just take any random frame from **THE BOXER'S OMEN** and freak out your strait-laced friends with its unbridled exploitive genius!

Kuei left the industry after his swan song, **MISFIRE** (走火炮 / *Zou huo pao*, 1984), to open a pizza joint in Orange County, California. He later died of liver failure. In my mind, he was one of the most important directors in Hong Kong cinema and put the Shaw Bros. studio on the map, because he wasn't afraid to use extreme supernatural violence to get a point across.

GHOST EYES is relatively tame compared to the aforementioned titles, but it has enough dread and creepiness to make up for it. This film has a sinister vibe even while nothing spooky is going on. They play this hair-raising music and use creative shot composition and camera angles…I really like the stylized quality.

This film revolves around a sharply dressed vampire named Mr. Shih (Szu Wei) and a mousy hairdresser named Pao-ling (Chen Szu-Chia). She accidentally breaks her eyeglasses. Since he's an optometrist, they set up an appointment for her to try on some contact lenses, which turns out to be code for "becoming Mr. Shih's eternal slave".

The intrusive pervy vampire, who resembles an Asian Jonathan Frid, has something even better than X-Ray Specs: he can hypnotize girls into getting naked against their will. It's the superpower that every pubescent boy secretly dreams of! Shih sets up Pao-ling with some sinister magical contact lenses, which cause her to see dead people. (I wonder if this inspired M. Night Shyamalan's shitty Bruce Willis vehicle?

Nah, **THE SIXTH SENSE** [1999] would've been way better if he'd been ripping off this movie.)

Soon Pao-ling learns that she can't pry the cursed contacts off her eyeballs. Maybe the LensCrafters corporation was trying to put the contact lens people out of business with this frightening bit of propaganda! Things start to get really freaky once she finds out that Mr. Shih's optical shop was burnt to the ground three years ago. Pao-ling decides to visit his grave and is almost sexually assaulted by a random drifter in the cemetery.

Mr. Shih has a ghostly grip of fear over her, and day by day the life is slowly sapped from her body. I feel sorry for Pao-ling—all she wanted was for someone to notice her and this two-bit ocular Dracula uses her emotional needs to take over her life and turn the salon into his feeding ground. Mr. Shih's evil stare can even drive innocent Pao-ling to kill others.

Mr. Shih searches for victims to replenish his yin and yang as well. The folklore in these Hong Kong horror films is very much unlike that of Western vampires, leaving out the classic "Van Helsing method". Instead of garlic and holy water, we get prayer flytrap scrolls and ritualistic magic. As an Asian-style vampire, Shih cannot be driven away by conventional Universal Studios Monster remedies. He isn't scared of a cross but lit incense keeps him away so he's probably Shinto or Buddhist or Wiccan or something.

Later on, his complexion goes from pasty white to a dark shade of moldy green and he froths at the mouth, fangs jutting out, like a typical vampire. The makeup is more reserved and not as messy as the director's other all-out gross-outs. Toward the end it gets pretty juicy, but nothing on a **SEEDING OF A GHOST** level of traumatic images.

Pao-ling escapes to a relative's house, but stalkers with supernatural powers aren't stopped that easily. Shih shows up whistling an eerie tune, which reminded me of Chris Sarandon in **FRIGHT NIGHT** (1985). Good thing Pao-ling's sister has plenty of incense. This pleasantly scented attack causes the monster's eyes to bug out and he degenerates into a demented Muppet! The film ends in an ambiguous way. We all know evil never dies; it just floats around for a while until it infects someone else!

GHOST EYES makes a strong argument against contact lenses. There's also important social commentary. Please, write to Congress and tell them that you support legislation to prevent bloodsucking madmen from taking advantage of those with an ocular handicap!

1974, HONG KONG. D: KUEI CHIH-HUNG
AVAILABLE FROM CELESTIAL PICTURES/
SHAW BROTHERS VIDEO

Russian poster for Freddie Francis' **CRAZE**

CRAZE
(a.k.a. **INFERNAL IDOL**, a.k.a. **DEMON MASTER**)

Reviewed by Steve Fenton

When is a monster movie *not* a monster movie? When it doesn't have anything even remotely resembling an actual monster in it, that's when! Simple, right? Or so you'd think, anyway. However, as everyone knows, life isn't always anywhere near so black-and-white nor cut-and-dried as that. And as art is often said to imitate life, why should *it* be either? Sometimes there is a good deal of ambiguity involved. There are borderline cases where a movie's monster can be more one of the mind than of the real physical world, yet still be classified as a monster of sorts in a very real sense. Case in point, the at-times crazed and always tawdrily trashy horror flick **CRAZE**, in my opinion. It makes for a strange beast indeed, simultaneously functioning as a demonic possession flick (hence the more monstrous content), yet also more marginally falling under the—horror of horrors!—"slasher" subgenre, in some respects. Indeed, I was so divided as to what category it most falls into (we do so love to pigeonhole things, don't we!) that I originally submitted a version of this review to *Weng's Chop*; however, having given the matter some further thought (as well as expanding on my original already long-winded

21

Chuku says "Fork you!"

review by another four- or five-hundred words!), I subsequently decided it might better fit the format of either *Monster!* digest or the upcoming *Monster! International* instead. But, wouldn't ya know, I've since opted to resubmit it for da *'Chop*'s horror-filled 2014 Spooktacular Special instead! So here goes nothin'…

Jack Palance (1919-2006) is one of those comparatively rare and gifted actors with an "offbeat" charisma and intense screen presence who has gotten a bad rep for being notoriously hammy at times; and it's justified, because he could be, and then some. But he could also be all-too-convincing in certain roles: as the ruthless gang boss in Elia Kazan's *noir* classic **PANIC IN THE STREETS** (1950), for instance; as a grizzled, no guts/no glory leatherneck infantry lieutenant in Robert Aldrich's take-no-prisoners WW2 epic **ATTACK!** (1956); or, perhaps most notably of all, as the pitiable washed-up, punch-drunk former champion pugilist in Ralph Nelson's riveting, Rod Serling-penned "Requiem for a Heavyweight" episode of the live TV drama series *Playhouse 90*, also produced in '56. Although he only ever appeared in comparatively few horror movies, some of those in which he did are real stand-outs, chiefly for his larger-than-life presence (as are a great many of his non-genre films as well, for that matter). He made a surprisingly effective Jekyll and a truly diabolical, Pan-like Hyde in Dan Curtis' classy Canadian-made teleplay *The Strange Case of Dr. Jekyll and Mr. Hyde* (1968), as well as a snarlingly sinister and physically intimidating yet at the same time dignified and sympathetic vampire lord in Curtis' fine 1974 made-for-TV adaptation of **DRACULA** (which was also released theatrically in numerous markets). Palance's work within the British horror genre included giving a convincingly hyper, jittery performance as an obsessed—and homicidal—literary fanboy in director Freddie Francis' own "The Man Who Collected Poe" segment of the underrated Robert Bloch-scripted Amicus omnibus **TORTURE GARDEN** (1968), in which his collecting rival was played by Peter Cushing, with whom the top-billed Palance interacts with winning onscreen chemistry. Which brings us to **CRAZE**, another thriller directed by Francis (1917-2007) in which Palance plays an unpredictable obsessive-compulsive character to fine—and sometimes quite frightening and/or hilarious—effect.

Of the mock-Hammer/Amicus/Tyburn stamp and produced by Herman **I WAS A TEENAGE WEREWOLF / FRANKENSTEIN** Cohen ([1925-2002] who co-wrote both those films and the present one's script with Aben Kandel [1897-1993]), **CRAZE** is one of the more obscure '70s Brit horrors which, having pretty much slipped through the cracks the first time round, remained largely unseen for decades (just for the record, this was my first viewing of it). Based on a presumably now difficult-to-find novel "of Witchcraft and Ritual Murder" by one Henry Seymour (*née* Helmut Henry Hartmann) entitled *Infernal Idol* (UK: Gifford, 1967; USA: Avon Books [#S400], 1969), the filmization received little fanfare at the time of its initial release, and most of the little I've ever heard or read about it has been negative and/or arbitrarily dismissive of the film, generally disregarding it as worthless trash. Trashy it most certainly is, but it definitely does have some worth for those willing to look for it, so don't be too quick to dismiss it sight unseen. If anybody's most likely to be forgiving towards such a film as this, it's a *Weng's Chop*per (or a *Monster!* maven, for that matter). Why, it's almost your *duty* to give it a fair shake, even if it is with a shit-dipped stick! If we champions of the world's cinematic dregs can't like it, who the fuck else is gonna?

I ask you, who among you can resist any movie that opens with a ritual in which a topless chick (alluring African-English starlet Venecia Day) dances deliriously before a grotesque pagan idol, waggling her arms and breasts at it with unbridled abandon (while Palance tries his best to keep a straight face!), then as a self-sacrificial gesture proceeds to slit her own belly open with a ceremonial dagger? Especially when this so-called "bloodletting" is accomplished in such a patently unconvincing manner using one of those phony prop knives that squirts stage blood without even so much as scratching her skin! (Granted, the dancer's demise appears to have been theatrically faked thus within the framework of the story, but this possibility is neither confirmed nor denied by the dialogue, and the woman's "corpse" is merely carted away by other cultists, never to be seen again, and we are left wondering what exactly went down.) Unfortunately, the bulk of **CRAZE** doesn't quite live up to the garish promise of this opening sequence, but it does have its moments and they don't come too few and far between, so you won't be lulled into snoozing.

The top-billed Palance appears as Neal Mottram, a professional London-based dealer in antiquities and amateur occultist who also happens to preside over—for wont of a better description, because the script is a little vague about the precise details—a cult of devil-worshipping practitioners of black magic. (Or it might well be a witches' coven, or both. Does the distinction really matter in such tawdry pulp fare as this anyway?) Evidently via less-than-above-board means, Palance has recently acquired possession of an ancient idol fashioned in the image of a regional African tribal deity named Chuku, which (who?) now squats atop an unholy altar in Palance's antique shop basement. When the disgruntled widow of its previous "rightful" owner comes a-calling demanding that the idol be handed over to her forthwith or else, during the ensuing struggle while fending the deranged woman off, she accidentally stumbles (*oops!*) smack-dab onto the razor-sharp metal tines of the vicious trident clutched in Chuku's immobile if not altogether lifeless hands. Shortly following the woman's demise, Palance comes into an unexpected windfall: about a thousand quid's worth of old gold coins, which he discovers stashed in a secret compartment of an antique bureau at his shop. Thus, the accidental death sets off a chain of events which lead to more and more "blood sacrifices", all made by Palance in the dark deity's name while he profits financially from the crimes due to Chuku's innate "generous" nature, whose bountifully bestowed rewards not surprisingly come with a steep price attached. In the interests of further filling his coffers, Palance goes about gladly

The sinister Chuku's got his evil eye (i.e., the *left* one) on you!

Cover to the '69 U.S. edition of the novel on which **CRAZE** was based

and gleefully filling his kill quota on cue at the devil god's behest. That's about the extent of the plot, and, while undeniably slim, there are far thinner ones around than what we have here.

According to the IMDb, the lead part had originally been written with an Englishman in mind, so presumably other than for his basic name value Palance, a Pennsylvanian of Ukrainian descent, wasn't the producers' ideal casting choice, and the actor at times appears to be putting on a fairly discreet English accent, albeit with a distinct American inflection (I suppose you might call it "Yanklish"?). Whatever's the case, all things considered given the rather outré storyline he does quite well in the part, playing it both understated and overwrought by turns as the script requires (when he roars "*You bluddy bahsturd!*" at one point in a pseudo-"Scotch" brogue definitely falls under the latter description). A self-professed Method actor, he really becomes immersed in the character. He has several explosively emotive—some might say hysterically histrionic—dramatic exchanges with his junior onscreen business associate (played by Martin Potter, best-known for the bizarre art-house peplum **FELLINI SATYRICON** [1969, Italy] and a lot lesser-known for Norman J. Warren's sexy shocker **SATAN'S SLAVE** [1976, UK]), a more youthfully ide-

alistic and ethical protégé who is evidently a reformed Hyde Park rent boy (i.e., "poofter") attempting to go straight in both meanings of the term. Some sort of still-ongoing homosexual relationship between the two men seems to be the implication, but this aspect isn't really delved into too deeply.

A goodly chunk of this movie's entertainment value is derived from spotting all the well-known faces which appear (and then disappear) throughout the running time, some of them only in glorified cameos and some for a couple of lengthier scenes, but the narrative's episodic structure guarantees that most of them get at least one meaty dialogue sequence in which to strut their stuff. Tops for me here was seeing buxotic überbird Diana Dors (1931-1984)—whom I always informally think of as "The Brit Shelley Winters"—as Dolly Newman, who runs a bed and breakfast, has a (quote) "weakness" for cherry brandy, wears a faux leopard-skin coat and indulges in a wham-bam-thank-you-ma'am one night stand just for old times' sake with her former flame, the Palance character, who's a bit of a Jack-the-lad about town, you see. Long after the glow has gone from her peach, Diana as Dolly says, "Hey, I don't want you to think I'm the sort who flops into bed with *any* Tom, Dick or 'arry!" and worries what her current betrothed—a hot-blooded Italian named Luigi—might do to her if he was to find out about her dalliance on the side while he was *in absentia* ("…one would have to be pretty desperate to sail into *that* port", remarks Michael Jayston's snotty dick of a dick about her at one point). Because she's such a naturalistic, seemingly effortless actress, you never doubt for a second that she isn't the characters she plays—that's how good she is. What a pity she passed away so young! I could easily imagine her in "stately" senior roles *à la* Helen Mirren or Judy Dench if she was still around today.

And speaking of stately seniors, in addition here we have no less than much-laureled English thespian Dame Edith Evans (1888-1976) making one of her final film appearances in her sole true horror movie as the unbalanced Palance's moneyed and highly ancient aunt. In one of the film's more outrageous scenes, in a bid to prematurely cash-in his inheritance at her expense he dons a creepy rubber fright mask—which is sort of meant to represent Chuku in his earthly manifestation, I suppose—in order to first scare the bejeezus out of the doddering old biddy, then carts her off into the garden of her palatial country estate, where he proceeds to (out-of-frame) shove a wooden stake into her as if killing a vampire. Another throwaway if nonetheless well-done sequence has Palance seeking the—*ahem*—hands-on services of a personal masseuse, played by the lovely, bright-eyed and perkily animated Suzy Kendall (top-billed the year previous on Sergio Martino's classic *giallo* **TORSO**, as well as filling the female lead role in Argento's

THE BIRD WITH THE CRYSTAL PLUMAGE in 1970). Kendall gives a charmingly earthy performance as saucy Sally the cash-on-the-barrelhead manhandler ("You name it, we have it; you need it, we use it!"), who keeps a closetful of black leather S/M gear at her ready disposal to service kinkier clients and utters such blatantly self-promotional come-ons as "The kind of massage I give is rather popular! Quite electrifying, in fact!" Adding a further wrinkle of good-humored sleaze to the proceedings, when Palance initially hires her services over the blower, he jots her number down on the topless centerfold of a skin-mag, whereafter she methodically pencils him into her busy datebook. Shortly upon arrival at her bedsit, Palance doesn't even bother availing himself of her recommended "Swedish massage" (which comes with a "double-voltage vibrator" chaser!) before—much more to her surprise than his—coldly and methodically murdering her via strangulation right while they are in the midst of a decidedly non-passionate liplock-turned-death kiss.

The bumper cast also includes the mighty Trevor Howard (1913-1988)—who appears scarcely able (or willing) to disguise his scorn for the material—as a gruff Scotland Yard superintendent who never steps foot out of the cop shop, allowing his subordinate played by Michael Jayston—who plays it like he thinks he's John Thaw as Regan in *The Sweeney!*—to handle the bulk of the investigation ("Quite the lady-killer, aren't you", remarks Jayston with some sarcasm regarding Palance's swinging lifestyle. "I do my share," replies Palance wryly). Sultry Norse sex goddess Julie Ege ([1943-2008] **CREATURES THE WORLD FORGOT, THE FREAKMAKER, THE LEGEND OF THE 7 GOLDEN VAMPIRES**) appears as Palance's first pub "pick-up", who winds up stuffed into a furnace by him and burned to the crispier side of well-done after their shared night of non-connubial bliss turns into one of sheer terror—albeit strictly one-sided on her part—when Chuku again gains the upper hand and incites his human puppet to commit another murder in his name. Percy Herbert ([1920-1992] **QUATERMASS II**) and David Warbeck ([1941-1997] **TWINS OF EVIL**) both play detectives on the case, and the great Welsh character actor/tippler Hugh Griffith ([1912-1980] **THE ABOMINABLE DR. PHIBES**) gets a throwaway bit-part as a mumbling solicitor. It's the kind of role he could easily have walked through in his sleep, and he might very well have been less than fully awake and/or sober when he read his lines, which were quite likely heavily lubricated for easier delivery by the potent potable of his choice.

CRAZE finally fully lives up to its title for the conclusion, when Palance—gone completely off his rocker due to the inhumanly evil compulsion which possesses him—takes a chopper to some coppers ("I'll chop you in half!"), leading into the downbeat denouement. As was seemingly director Francis' express intention, it never is definitely determined, at

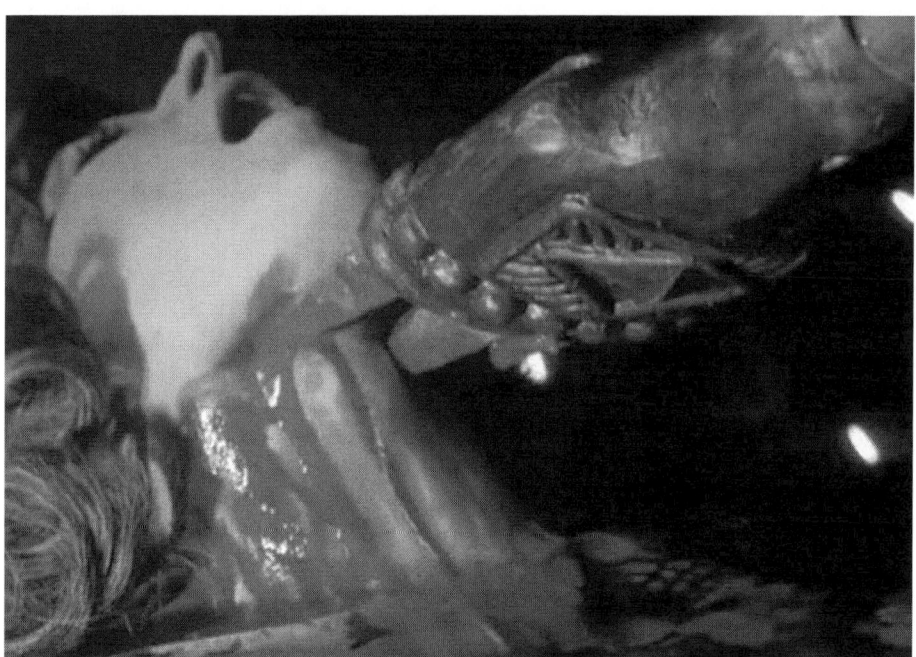

Weng's Chop promises not to make a tasteless "She's forked!" joke to go with this screen capture from **CRAZE**, okay?

least verbally within the script, whether Palance's homicidal behavior genuinely stems from the infernal idol's dark influence, or if it is all only part of some purely personal delusional mania from which he is suffering (this hypothesis seems to be borne out by the title, which just might imply that it is all only in his mind…or *is* it?!). So, although things may have been a good deal more entertaining had the static statue of Chuku come impossibly to life and gone around laying waste to an expendable extra or two with that jugular-jabbing pitchfork of his, such a development might have been a little too literal to suit Francis, who seemed to be striving for more subtly psychological ramifications rather than have us take things too literally. I'd be interested in reading the reportedly quite well-written original source novel to see how its author handled the psychology of the main character. As it is, what we are left with is a satisfyingly sensationalistic slice of horror trashola of the most entertaining kind, so by all means give it a gander.

For all the basic ambiguity as to whether actual supernatural forces are at work and whether Palance as Mottram is indeed under some sort of otherworldly influence or not, I prefer to read it as a "legitimate" depiction of diabolic possession; after all, what other explanation but a paranormal one could there possibly be for all those "unexpected" riches Palance's character comes into shortly following each new murder? Chalking it all up to mere coincidence would be more far-fetched than attributing it to actual acts of supernatural intervention! For this reason, I prefer to believe that the infernal internal intelligence which Palance believes resides within the far-from-idle idol is an actual entity with a tangible earthly existence: an invisible puppet master, if you will, pulling the strings of those who fall under its thrall and manipulating them like marionettes for malevolent ends. Just for the sake of some "subtle" symbolic contrast, a benign Buddha statue is seen in some shots, and just to drive home the symbolism is even framed in C/U (albeit only in profile) for one shot. Making for an oddly imposing presence, the graven image of Chuku himself/itself is shot from a plethora of skewed and distorted "*Batman*" angles to better capture his/its innate evil character; and this is conveyed so well by the cinematography that it at times appears as if Chuku is indeed a tangibly alive, sentient entity. Hence, it's a cinch to imagine the bugger springing to literal life…which might quite likely happen by virtue of CG technology if **CRAZE** was ever to be remade in this modern age (after all the from-out-of-left-field remakes we've seen in recent years, don't entirely rule out the possibility of it happening!). But if they did remake it and Chuku suddenly turned into Chucky and started running around slaughtering people right, left and center while delivering witty one-liners, that might definitely tax our suspension of disbelief, even if it would likely make things a good deal more entertaining.

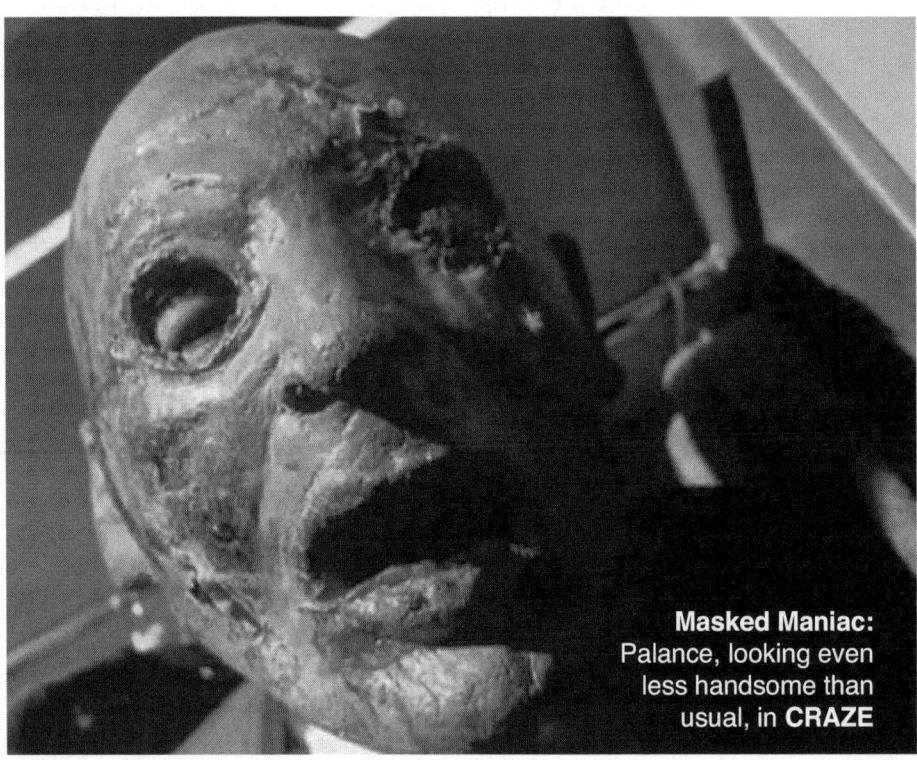

Masked Maniac: Palance, looking even less handsome than usual, in **CRAZE**

Now if only a nice quality edition of this flick would turn up on disc! Having recently watched sumptuously presented disc versions of such previously oft-maligned '60s/'70s Brit shockers as **IT** (a.k.a. **CURSE OF THE GOLEM**), **THE BLOOD BEAST TERROR** (a.k.a. **THE VAMPIRE-BEAST CRAVES BLOOD**) and **TROG**, all of which were far easier to take simply due to the vivid clarity of their new incarnations' presentation, this further confirms that even the lowlier specimens of cinécrud can be boosted a few notches higher on the quality scale when viewed at their correct aspect ratio in top-of-the-line, state-of-the-art transfer prints.

That said, the copy of **CRAZE** up at YouTube which I watched for the purposes of this review was ripped from an indeterminate source (tape? TV? a 16mm film chain?) and is of exceedingly poor quality: full frame pan-and-scan with washed-out, virtually non-existent color and very muggy, distorted sound which sometimes faded-out to the point where it became virtually inaudible and unintelligible (thus making Palance's sometimes mumbling delivery of his lines all the harder to make sense of!). But if I could enjoy the film nonetheless even under such piss-poor conditions as those, I'm sure I'd like it that much better if it were presented in a more optimal format. Some months following my first exposure to the film, I did a new search for a better copy at YT, and—lo and behold—someone (bless 'em!) had been kind enough to upload a much more user-friendly rip; although also full-frame, this version has much better picture quality, with far nicer color and clearer contrast too (even if it does fluctuate occasionally, as though more than one version have been cut-together). And now for the bad news: said nicer-quality version since seems to have vanished from YT, I'm sorry to say. The only English-language versions which remained up there as of this writing were all evidently ripped from the same shoddy source as the one I originally watched.

NOTES: I think those aforementioned YT uploads may have been ripped(-off) from the reportedly horrendous copy of **CRAZE** included in BCI/Eclipse's ultra-cheap NTSC Region 1 DVD horror collection "Slasher Cinema" (which also includes **THE DEMON** and **THE GLOVE** [both 1979] and **MEMORIAL VALLEY MASSACRE** [1988]). There are apparently two far superior German DVD editions available from X-Rated Kult and KNM Home Entertainment[2], and the special features of either one or both of those discs include some "bonus" scenes of Palance as Mottram interacting with "his" Chuku idol. Digivision of Italy has also issued **CRAZE** on PAL Region 2 disc, again in full-screen format rather than at its proper original theatrical aspect ratio of 1.85:1 (I'm gonna go out on a limb here and assume

their edition comes with an English audio and/or softsubs option).[3] Back in the '80s, the film received at least two domestic North American VHS videocassette releases (from the dreaded, rock-bottom Saturn Productions and another company called VCR).

1974, UK. D: FREDDIE FRANCIS
AVAILABLE FROM X-RATED KULT [R2, OOP]

THE SPACE CHILDREN

Reviewed by Steve Fenton

Ad-line: *"All the children on Earth enslaved by the thing from outer space..."*
Dialogue quote: *"Is there no man on Earth who has the wisdom and innocence of a child?"*

This was reportedly director Jack Arnold's personal favorite of his handful of sturdy, generally well-regarded '50s SF classics, which also included the first two *Creature* features, plus **IT CAME FROM OUTER SPACE** (1953), **TARANTULA** (1955), **THE INCREDIBLE SHRINKING MAN** (1957) and 1958's **MONSTER ON THE CAMPUS** (that lattermost title reputedly being Arnold's least favor-

---

2 Both, now OOP but still obtainable from secondary market sources as of this writing, are presented in an open-matte 1.33:1 aspect ratio. *–ed.*

3 Also OOP but still obtainable (reportedly presented in the same open-matte full-frame), but be warned: according to *dvdcompare. net*, this release is missing some footage, although, apparently, not for censorship reasons. By most accounts, as of this writing the X-Rated Kult release seems the way to go if you want to obtain this title for your collection. *–ed.*

Brainchild: Sandy Descher and Michel Ray [third and fourth from left], with the rest of **THE SPACE CHILDREN**, in a specially-posed publicity shot from the film

ite fantasy offering of all his repertory). Ironically enough, although **THE SPACE CHILDREN** (1958) was the director's fave within his canon, it is his least well-known and most seldom-seen genre entry. With its ultimate anti-war message, it basically reworks the germ of the original idea behind Robert Wise's **THE DAY THE EARTH STOOD STILL** (1951, USA), albeit rearranging and outright changing the specifics considerably along the way. But the ultimate message of the two films is highly similar.

As per the present film's title, the mixed-gender juvenile progeny of scientists working on a top-secret U.S. space project encounter a gigantic, glowing extraterrestrial brain in a seaside cave close by to the launching site. Yes, it's every bit as good as it sounds!

A kind of early precursor to the so-called "Star Wars" project, the scientists' hush-hush work at the Eagle Point Missile Project entails the development and construction of a rocket dubbed the "Thunderer," which, if all goes well (it *doesn't*, of course) will have the capability of shuttling a satellite equipped with a hydrogen bomb into orbit to serve as a ready deterrent to the other global superpowers from pushing the button. According to one of the project's top eggheads Dave Brewster, "In all its history, our country's never started a war. The Thunderer's *to prevent war*".

The families dwell in a trailer park near to the premises, where they engage in such wholesomely down-homey all-American activities as weenie roasts and keeping up with the Joneses. While life goes on as usual at the test complex, an eerie tractor beam from outer space deposits the brain down to Earth. Shortly thereafter, having discovered its whereabouts, seven preteens, led by Bud Brewster (the top-billed Michel Ray) and Edie (Sandy Descher), fall under the mental thrall of the invading interplanetary cerebrum, whose intentions remain as-yet unclear, but are presumably sinister or even outright malevolent. When first seen roughly the size of an ostrich egg, the brain-being soon grows to outlandish proportions, glowing with an eerie inner illumination and pulsing rhythmically.

Besides this film, another of juvenile star Ray's best-known roles was as a Mexican *chico* in Irving Rapper's family drama **THE BRAVE ONE** (1956, USA). The future Ty Hardin (*née* Hungerford, also seen in Gene Fowler, Jr.'s eerie **I MARRIED A MONSTER FROM OUTER SPACE** that same year) appears in a bit part as a base security officer posted at the front gate. Former **ATTACK OF THE CRAB MONSTERS** co-star and future *Gilligan's Island* cast member Russell "The Professor" Johnson (who passed away this past January) appears as a self-pitying/-loathing alcoholic slacker stepfather named Joe Gamble, who's pretty much a waste of both air and space. As if by some wrathful retributory act of God, his angrily abusive character is zapped by a bolt of telekinetic extraterrestrial energy when he dares to raise a hand in anger against his stepson, who is one of the kids under the alien intellect's control and protection.

Early attempts by the children during moments of lucidity ("It fell out of the sky") fall on deaf ears, as, needless to say, their parents and other adults are skeptical of their tall tale. However, due to his sons Bud and Ken, Dr. Brewster is made privy to the kids' secret, which remains in hiding in its cave lair down at the beach. Brewster attempts to warn the project heads, only to be mentally "influenced" by the brain so that he physically loses his voice and is unable to divulge the alien's existence to anyone.

Although made at a time when the Cold War was still very much in full force, as though to not risk baiting any outside aggressor, specific mention of either the U.S.S.R. or Red China is not made, with the potential hostile foreign power being simply tactfully referred to as "another country". One of the scientists on the project—played by Raymond Bailey—is symbolically named Dr. Wahrmann ("war-man"… get it?). No sooner has the countdown ended than the Thunderer really lives up to its name by getting blown sky-high; if by no means in the way it was intended to. This development leads into the downbeat conclusion, which is surprising without really coming as much of a surprise whatsoever…but I mean that in a *good* way.

Rather than maliciously malignant "cuckoos" *à la* those in Wolf Rilla's masterful **VILLAGE OF THE DAMNED** (1960, UK), the children here are benign beings, serving as compliant pawns to the passive-aggressive alien intellect. Even with all its lofty aims to elevate kids' lowly social status ("We're in the power of the children"…"The children have *won*!"), one can only wonder how this film might have fared with juvenile moviegoers of its day. Its naïvely idealistic/optimistic ending has kids all around the world uniting to oppose the international arms race, and **THE SPACE CHILDREN** closes with a pertinent Biblical quote, laid against a heavenly star-field.

Although for the purposes of this review I watched a good ol' VHS copy taped off network TV sometime back in the '90s, the film is available on Blu-ray and DVD, so it shouldn't be too hard to track down a copy. If you're in any way, shape or form a lover of 'Fifties sci-fi, you need to own this in at least *some* format.

1958, USA. D: JACK ARNOLD
AVAILABLE FROM OLIVE FILMS

THE LEECH WOMAN

Reviewed by Steve Fenton

A sensationalistic quote from the original trailer: *"For Her There Could Be No Love, Only Endless Horror!"*

Like **THE BRAIN EATERS** (1958) and **THE CORPSE GRINDERS** (1971), here we have a classic exploitation movie title that conjures up all kinds of bizarre, slimy imagery in the mind's eye (it presumably provided either direct or at least indirect inspiration for the disgusting "leech woman" doll seen in Full Moon's *Puppet Master* movie franchise of the '80s/'90s and beyond). As for the present film itself though, it is rather run-of-the-mill; a pretty typical late-'50s shocker, but given the Universal treatment, which lent even that studio's sleaziest lower-budget items—this is very definitely one of them—at the very least a sheen of professional mediocrity. While the look and setting couldn't be more dissimilar, in its base premise **THE LEECH WOMAN** (1960) seems to have been inspired by Hammer Films' quest-for-eternal-life yarn **THE MAN WHO COULD CHEAT DEATH** (1959, UK), starring Anton Diffring as a male counterpart of Coleen Gray's character herein.

The aptly-named Ms. Gray—whose surname here matches her hair color—portrays the title "critter", actually just a vain, aging if independently wealthy woman desperate to cling to her fading (um, better make that *faded*) youth and beauty, but by now well past it and into her fifties…at least, judging by the looks of her, anyway (her actual age is never men-

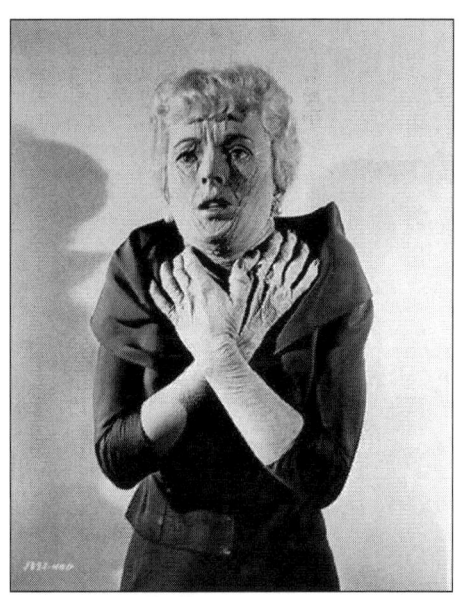

Age Before Beauty: Coleen Gray as **THE LEECH WOMAN**

tioned, but she's well beyond the simple mudpack and Oil of Olay touch-up stage, that's for sure). Thanks to an ancient native witch-woman named Malla (the exceedingly crinkly-wrinkly and scrawny Estelle Hemsley, a living mummy who's only 152 but looks about 200 if she's a day), our over-the-hill, gone-to-seed and out-to-pasture antiheroine discovers a way of rejuvenating herself while in Tanganyika, Africa: this via a potent potion called Nypee ("a hormone which retards aging"), which is distilled by members of a native tribe called the Nando, who guard their secret jealously, killing all interlopers who attempt to make off with this forbidden knowledge. The main ingredients in Nypee's distillation are pollen from a rare species of orchid, as well as another vital part of the recipe: namely essence of pineal gland, forcibly taken from the base of a living human's neck, thus causing the involuntary donor's instant demise.

Suffering from low self-esteem due to her perceived lack of desirability and eager to recapture her lost youth and attractiveness, following her first "treatment", Gray learns the hard way that she must thereafter constantly seek out new victims in order to prevent herself from succumbing to the horrible effects of accelerated aging and…death. And the intervals between treatments seem to become shorter and shorter each time, meaning that she requires an ever-increasing supply to feed her voracious vanity. With each new relapse she gets progressively crinklier. After missing her crucial dosage of gland-juice, much to her horror she succumbs to sudden advanced decrepitude. By now well past her expiry date, she takes her own life by leaping from a window to the sidewalk far below rather than face her ugly mug, which—much like Dorian Gray's deteriorating portrait—not only reminds her of her physical decrepitude, which shows on the outside, but her still uglier moral corruption too, which shows even clearer (if beauty is indeed only skin-deep, ugliness can often go a good deal deeper).

THE LEECH WOMAN is an entertaining, albeit somewhat sordid search-for-eternal-youth yarn, featuring some vicious psychological torture, cold-hearted murder, lots of mean-spirited human lowlifes, and a good helping of thinly-veiled '50s sexual innuendo in the dialogue. Many of the familiar canned "jungle" sound FX heard here were also used in slews of other Unipix from the period, so overall this makes for a highly familiar package, albeit with a couple of startling surprises in store; even if I did give the ending away again, but it doesn't come as much of a surprise anyway, because it's about what we've been expecting considering the formulaically predictable material. Though strictly "B"-league in format and execution, things are elevated above the usual dreck by usual glamor girl-turned-figurative parasitic annelid-hag Ms. Gray's assured performance, which is far better than such comparatively lowly material warranted. Along much the same lines as Corman's THE WASP WOMAN (1959)—if a good deal more grim and grimy and played with a completely straight face, unlike said Corman film—this is a nice retro reprise of familiar "glandular extract" shockers from the previous decade, like Universal's own **THE MAD GHOUL** (1943) and PRC's **THE MONSTER MAKER** (1944 [see *Monster!* digest #7]), that latter item being one of the grimmest, most cynical and meanest-spirited horror efforts of the entire 'Forties, with the former running it a close second in the man's-inhumanity-to-man stakes.

In the present film, Gray is involved in a loveless marriage-of-convenience (i.e., *his*) to a selfish and opportunistic gigolo endocrinologist, Dr. Paul Talbot (Philip Terry), who is conducting expensive if unsuccessful research into reversing—and quite possibly even eliminating entirely—the aging process. Their rocky marital relations are further exacerbated by his (quote) "bottle baby" wife's acute alcoholism, which he constantly rubs her nose in in a most reprehensible manner indeed; although there is definitely a good deal of bitter truths to be found in some of the (in)human nature displayed herein. During one spiteful spat the hateful hubby hits his fast-fading spouse where it hurts most by saying, "Old women always give me the creeps!" This "ageist" remark amounts to only one instance of misanthropic sentiment in a film which includes plenty. Very few of its characters display many—if any—honorable traits, and most harbor sneaky—even slimy—ulterior motives of some sort. Purely in the interests of squeezing his lawfully-wedded but despised wife for more cash, her self-serving, emotionally manipulative hubby convinces her to call off their divorce plans by cruelly playing on her all-too-sincere love for him (the only person he loves is *himself*!). Having been thus routinely used and abused, when the time comes for her to reclaim her lost beauty, she thinks nothing of utilizing her husband's pineal gland to prepare her first draught of Nypee, killing him in the process. Playing their seedy jungle guide Bertram Garvay, Germanic actor John Van Drelen in turn steals "the elixir of sudden wealth and beauty" off Gray after she has only just stolen it from the natives. While they are making good their getaway from the Nando village through the jungle, Van Drelen falls into a swamp and is about to go under while Gray stands idly by, disdainfully indifferent to his plight. If he wants her to save him, Gray demands that he fork over the filched Nypee forthwith, or it's curtains for him. No sooner has he done so and she has dragged him from the morass than she (non-graphically) rips out his precious pineal—which she considers of more value to her than to him—by means of a special hooked ring she wears on her finger.

No actual transformation scenes are included showing the actress' advancing and receding decrepitude, although the haggard, wizened makeup job while she is in her more aged format is very well-done for the time (coming years prior to legendary makeup maestro Dick Smith's pioneering work in the field of old-age prosthetics on Arthur Penn's revisionist Hollywood Western **LITTLE BIG MAN** [1970], starring Dustin Hoffman as the title character). For the purposes of stark contrast in the present film, in her temporarily rejuvenated state when all her sexual confidence returns in spades and she becomes an irresistible man-magnet once more, Gray radiates a prettiness and vivacity far removed from her mopey, morose older alter-ego, which makes for a more dramatic contrast between her two separate selves (essentially what we have here is still another variant on the much-used "Jekyll/Hyde" split personality concept). Indeed, Gray does such a fine job in her dual role(s) that at times her young and old alter-egos seem to have been played by different actresses rather than both by the same one. When in younger mode, Gray poses as her own fictitious, flirtatious niece, Terri Hart, who gives flimsy throwaway explanations for her so-called aunt's "sudden disappearances" from the picture whenever she's around. She then turns on her yummiliciously youthful charms and attempts to put the make on wholesomely hunky hero Grant Williams (previously seen in his most famous role as **THE INCREDIBLE SHRINKING MAN** [1957], as well as playing the male lead of the offbeat mineral alien invasion flick **THE MONOLITH MONSTERS** [1958]; both those films were also Universal-International productions). However, Williams' onscreen fiancée played by popular '50s psychotronic starlet Gloria Talbott (heroine of **DAUGHTER OF DR. JEKYLL** and **THE CYCLOPS** [both 1957; see *Monster!* digest #6 for

Belgian poster for **THE LEECH WOMAN**

31

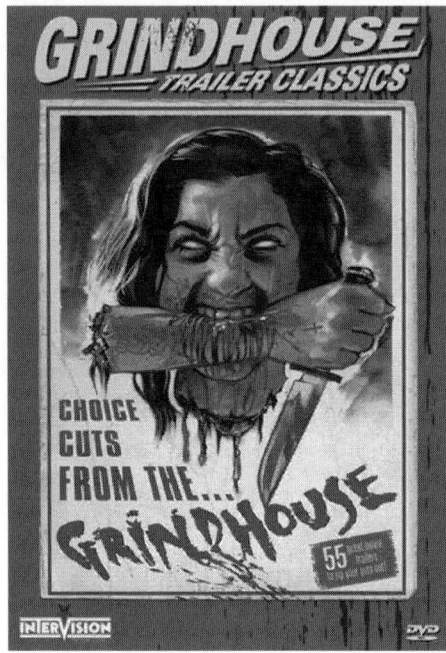

A good deal nastier but with more of a sense of humor to temper its nastiness, **THE REJUVENATOR** (a.k.a. **THE REJUVENATRIX**, 1988, USA) is a far more fanciful and gorily outrageous later variation on a similar well-trod theme.

1960, USA. D: EDWARD DEIN
AVAILABLE FROM UNIVERSAL STUDIOS HOME ENTERTAINMENT

GRINDHOUSE TRAILER CLASSICS

Reviewed by Brian Harris

The trailer compilation is nothing new; there are scores of compilations out there—many released by dodgy bootleg companies or defunct labels—but it wasn't until around 2005 that we here in the States received a steady stream of high quality trailers in the form of Synapse Films' popular **42nd STREET FOREVER** DVD series, launched in 2005. Two years later, our cult cinema counterparts in the UK received their very own trailer series entitled **GRINDHOUSE TRAILER CLASSICS**, thanks to Jake West (**EVIL ALIENS** [2005], **PUMPKINHEAD: ASHES TO ASHES** [2006]), Marc Morris and their cult/horror label, Nucleus Films. Here we are seven years later and Nucleus have released three more volumes (**VOLUME 2** [2008], **VOLUME 3** [2011], and **VOLUME 4** [2014]). This is just the **GRINDHOUSE TRAILER CLASSICS** series, not their insanely popular **VIDEO NASTIES: THE DEFINITIVE GUIDE** series, which also features trailers and fantastic documentaries. I'll be touching on the **VIDEO NASTIES: THE DEFINITIVE GUIDE** (Volume 1) in the next issue of *WC*. While Nucleus's series may not be as prolific as Synapse's, it easily parallels it in quality. Don't take my word for it, though, grab a copy and check it out for yourselves!

Oh, you don't own a region free disc player, you say?

Luckily for you, Severin Films—releasing under their InterVision Picture Corp. imprint—have not only picked up Nucleus' **VIDEO NASTIES: THE DEFINITIVE GUIDE** (Volume 1) but they also picked up and released **GRINDHOUSE TRAILER CLASSICS** (Volume 1)! Now you can enjoy what the lucky sleazehounds out in the UK have been raving about! Can this bit o' information get any better? Sure can: Severin have also secured the rights to release volumes 2-4 of the **GRINDHOUSE TRAILER CLASSICS** series, as well as the second volume in the **VIDEO NASTIES: THE DEFINITIVE GUIDE** series! Sexy, right? So what in the hell is in this awesome DVD and which trailers convinced you to purchase something? Here's what we get:

I DRINK YOUR BLOOD (1970), **I EAT YOUR SKIN** (1964), **BLOOD SPATTERED BRIDE** (1972), **I DIS-**

a review of that latter title]), takes exception to this sexy blonde young upstart/cuckoo from out of left field attempting to horn-in on her territory and oust her from his affections, and stands by her man jealously until the end…which proves to be her own, not Gray's (whose own undoing shortly follows, as described above). An impulsive crime of passion precipitates the lurid denouement, ending things on a suitably downbeat note…not that after all the miserable misanthropy which has preceded it we were expecting a happy ending, by any means. Of course, when compared to some of the stuff that's around these days, **THE LEECH WOMAN** is positively small potatoes when it comes to nastiness; but if you place the film into the proper perspective of the time in which it was produced—right on the cusp of when the '50s became the '60s—it registers as quite the nasty piece of work indeed, simply by comparison to most of what was around at that time.

By no means cheerful trash, but effective in its own bleak way, this was long one of Uni's harder to track down titles (another still more elusive one for the longest time was **THE THING THAT COULDN'T DIE** [1959; see *Weng's Chop* #4], which has finally become a lot more easy to see in recent years, for better or worse). The present film eventually became readily available as one of the ten titles included in Universal's multiple-disc "The Classic Sci-Fi Ultimate Collection" Region 1 boxed DVD set (issued in 2008); although this standard pulp horror tale's science-fictional elements are decidedly minimal…try next to nonexistent.

MEMBER MAMA (1972), **SWITCHBLADE SISTERS** (1975), **CAGED HEAT** (1974), **EYEBALL** (1975), **DERANGED** (1974), **THE BIG DOLL HOUSE** (1971), **BURY ME AN ANGEL** (1972), **LAST HOUSE ON THE LEFT** (1972), **THE STREETFIGHTER** (1974), **ILSA – SHE WOLF OF THE SS** (1974), **DR. BLACK, MR. HYDE** (1976), **DON'T OPEN THE WINDOW** (1974), **THE HUMAN TORNADO** (1976), **CAGED VIRGINS** (1971), **EBONY, IVORY & JADE** (1979), **DEADLY WEAPONS** (1974), **TORSO** (1973), **THEY CALL HER ONE EYE** (1973), **DEATH SHIP** (1980), **MASTER OF THE FLYING GUILLOTINE** (1976), **THEY CAME FROM WITHIN** (1975), **THE THING WITH TWO HEADS** (1972), **I SPIT ON YOUR GRAVE** (1978), **SWEET SUGAR** (1972), **GIRLS FOR RENT** (1974), **THE TOOLBOX MURDERS** (1978), **THE EXECUTIONER** (1978), **HOUSE OF WHIPCORD** (1974), **TRUCK TURNER** (1974), **GOD TOLD ME TO** (1976), **DOCTOR BUTCHER M.D.** (1980), **CHILDREN SHOULDN'T PLAY WITH DEAD THINGS** (1972), **NIGHT OF THE BLOODY APES** (1969), **BLOODSUCKING FREAKS** (1976), **ILSA – HAREM KEEPER OF THE OIL SHEIKS** (1976), **THE SINGLE GIRLS** (1974), **THE CORPSE GRINDERS** (1971), **ZOMBIE** (1979), **COFFY** (1973), **THE PERILS OF GWENDOLINE** (1984), **LEGEND OF THE WOLF WOMAN** (1977), **SATAN'S SADISTS** (1969), **DISCO GODFATHER** (1979), **LET ME DIE A WOMAN** (1977), **THE DOLL SQUAD** (1973), **SECRETS OF SWEET SIXTEEN** (1973), **CANNONBALL** (1976), **AUTOPSY** (1975), **FIGHT FOR YOUR LIFE** (1977), **LOVE ME DEADLY** (1973), **WHAM! BAM! THANK YOU, SPACEMAN** (1975), **SHOGUN ASSASSIN** (1980), **THREE ON A MEATHOOK** (1973).

Along with the trailers—which all look beautiful—we also get a cool poster gallery featuring posters for all of the films whose trailers are featured, as well as a short (18min. 30sec.) featurette entitled "Bump 'N' Grind: Emily Booth Explores The World of The Grindhouse", hosted by steaming hot actress and UK television personality, Emily Booth. The featurette is fun, informative and sexy as hell; a nice little extra to be sure. Those who don't know anything about the grindhouse or its history will certainly receive enough info to hit the Internet and start flame wars over who has more grindhouse knowledge "e-cred".

While I must admit to owning quite a few of the films featured on this disc, I still love watching the trailers, as they provide viewers of today with a small glimpse into the era these films were made, like minute-and-a-half time capsules. Ultimately, the goal of the trailer though is to convince you to watch a film, and if it doesn't work a trailer is useless and there's no love lost, time spent or money blown on your end. I'm pleased to say, the trailer for **LOVE ME DEADLY** did its job and I'm determined to own and see it, even if it doesn't live up to its salacious trailer.

So, if you're a trailer compilation fan, such as myself, you're going to want to grab **GRINDHOUSE TRAILER CLASSICS**. You may own a few other comps that feature many of the same trailers but that probably won't stop you, just as it didn't stop me. Great pick-up, Severin!

2007, UK. FEATURETE DIRECTOR: JAKE WEST
AVAILABLE FROM INTERVISION/SEVERIN FILMS

National Theatre Live's

FRANKENSTEIN

Reviewed by Kris Gilpin

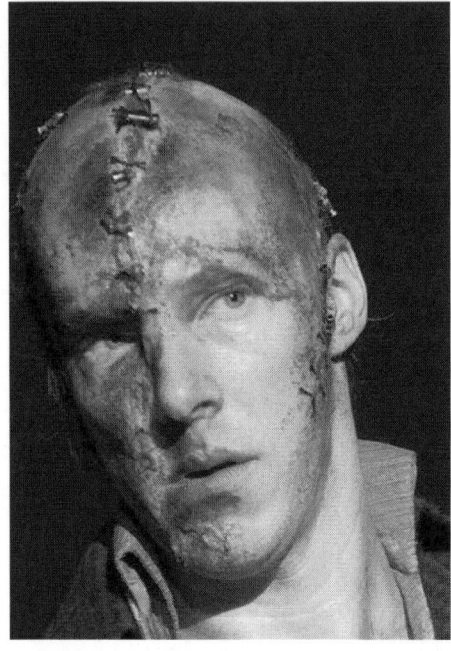

I stupidly missed this *Frankenstein* in Salt Lake City when it first came out, beat myself up for that, and had to wait three more years to see it Halloween week in Florida. It stars two modern Sherlocks, Benedict (**STAR TREK: INTO THE DARKNESS** [2013]) Cumberbatch as the Creature and Jonny Lee (**TRAINSPOTTING** [1996], **DARK SHADOWS** [2012]) Miller as the scientist, with the actors switching their roles in a second, alternate version of this filmed stage play. I love some of these Fathom Events presentations, like the always funny *RiffTrax*, MST3K-like live bad-movie shows, and *The Curious Incident of the Dog in the Night-Time* (which was a great book!).

The film started with some production stills and the short documentary, *Creating Frankenstein*, narrated by Danny Boyle (**TRANCE** [2013]) who filmed this live production—which I believe was directed onstage by Nicholas Hytner (**THE MADNESS OF KING GEORGE** [1994]) and Nick Dear, the show's writer—who tells how he stuck to the novel and not the Karloff classic, which was told thru the doctor's point of view, and basically just had the creature grunt. Dear made his Frankenstein's monster the star, gave him dialogue, intelligence and longing (though of course he's not an innocent), as the mad doctor himself (and Miller is in fine form here, too) makes his first major appearance about 40 minutes into the show.

Naomie Harris is the Frankenstein fiancé—I thought she was so beautiful under all that make-up in **PIRATES OF THE CARIBBEAN: DEAD MAN'S CHEST** (2006)—and the good, eclectic music is by Underworld (whose side group, Freur, made some *great* pop rock!), which Boyle—or was it Hytner?—used to score the production like a film.

Cumberbatch gives a typically great, twitchy performance, spending the first 10 or so minutes being birthed from a cell-like membrane, as he groans, flops around in baby-like pantomime and then learns to walk. His make-up of stitches is good, too.

A huge chandelier made of hundreds of tiny lights bulbs hangs above the stage (the production values are all impressively quirky), most of the show is dark, and there are some shocks and blood on display.

There is some very good, smart dialogue between Cumberbatch and Miller, and Benedict and Naomie, when their characters first meet. I wished so badly I could have gone back two nights later to watch/compare the version with Miller as the Creature and Cumberbatch as Victor, but I'm still hoping for a double Blu-ray soon (with hopefully director/actors' commentary!).[1] It's a great adaptation with some great acting.

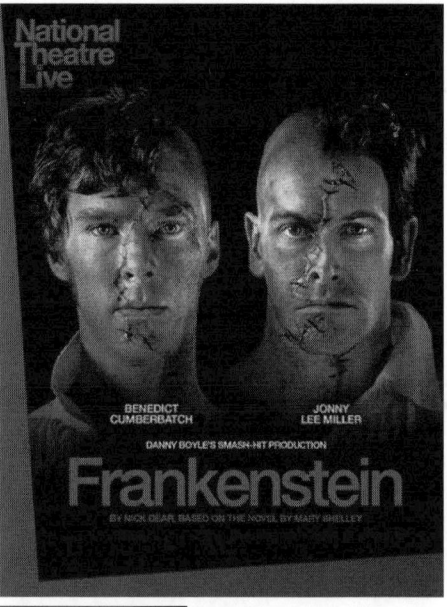

[1] Sadly, the creators of this production have been very vocal about their vehement desire to keep this filmed play from *ever* being released on home video, intending instead to make it an annual limited theatrical engagement. Let's hope they change their minds at some point. *–ed.*

INTERVIEWS

LESSONS IN DETERMINATION:
A CONVERSATION WITH DANIEL STAMM

by Art Stevenson

German filmmaker Daniel Stamm is perhaps a writer-director most closely associated with the horror genre, but when **Weng's Chop** magazine spoke with him we found a filmmaker who was more in love with both a good story and good characters as opposed to this single genre.

The primary reason we were talking was his latest feature **13 SINS (2014)**, but in a thoroughly immersive conversation Stamm took us on a journey from his childhood in Germany where he discovered his inspiration, through the terrifying loneliness of Stamm the writer, and on to Hollywood and his foray into **THE LAST EXORCISM (2010)** and **13 SINS**. The conversation possessed an air of honesty that took us behind the scenes of the American filmmaking machine to see how the cogs work, whilst also possessing an acceptance to the inevitable difference between American and European filmmaking—two different animals that belong to the same family.

Why a career in filmmaking? Was there that one inspirational moment?

I grew up in Germany where I was a Boy Scout. Someone at some point brought in this role playing game, Dungeons and Dragons, which blew my mind. Just the idea that a couple of people could sit around a table and come up with something out of thin air that would suddenly exist for everyone, and where you were a god of your own fictional world with your own fictional characters that people would care so much about. It was so much so that if a fictional character died they would break down into tears. I just knew that I wanted to do that professionally somehow.

At first not wanting to let go of that feeling I wanted to be a writer and come up with stories. In Germany we first need a diploma from a university, and besides my parents would never have let me do something where I didn't first have to go to university to study. So I was looking around for writing programmes, and one of the ones that seemed to be the best was the screenwriting programme. So I ended up at film school, although I didn't want to make movies, I just wanted to write.

How did the transition into filmmaking occur?

My friends went off with my scripts and made them only to come back with these amazing stories from the set—these war stories. I felt so left out because I was sitting in my little room plotting my scripts, and I always had the feeling that the storytelling process was artificially cut into two halves. If I had written the story and I had already played it all in my head then I didn't need someone else to come in and take over to communicate that to the cinematographer, the production designer and the actors—I could do that myself.

So after finishing the writing programme I moved to Los Angeles where I studied directing. Since then I have directed horror films, although I never necessarily thought of myself as a horror person.

I had just made my first film with a couple of friends on a video camera, and the producers of **THE LAST EXORCISM** along with Eli Roth wanted that same documentary style. I had never made horror before, but they invited me in and asked, "Can you make a horror movie in that style?" I had already learned that in Hollywood you always say yes whenever somebody asks you to do something. You first say yes and then on your way back you think oh my God, what did I get myself into? [Laughs] They don't deal well with our European understatement of never wanting to over-promise something. Instead they want someone who doesn't hesitate and says, "Of course I can do it." Then you have to figure it out later, and that's what happened with **THE LAST EXORCISM**, which I got into very quickly, and where I found myself suddenly terrified at the prospect of having to direct a horror movie.

How did the approach to and experience of directing THE LAST EXORCISM influence your approach to 13 SINS?

If you look at **THE LAST EXORCISM** it's not that much of a horror movie—it's more of a character study and drama. But it was sold as this big horror movie with an horrific trailer and poster, and suddenly I was a horror guy. In Hollywood most people don't actually watch the movie—they look at the box office numbers and the people involved, which in my case was Eli. So that immediately branded me a horror guy, and so I found myself suddenly receiving all of these horror scripts.

It is really hard to break out of that, and I don't even need to break out of it—I just need to find original material that is interesting. But in horror it is so hard to do something original because people want certain cornerstones within their stories, which you have to hit, and which we didn't hit with **THE LAST EXORCISM**. The audience was left disappointed, and as much as a box office success as it was, the audience hated it because they had been sold a different movie to the one that they had brought their tickets to see. I didn't want to do the same thing with **13 SINS**, and as I knew it was going to be a Dimension movie it was going to be sold as a bloody, gory, gruesome film. So I thought for the people who respond to that marketing and want to see that type of film, then why don't we give it to them? But then we tried to also put everything that we wanted to do in terms of character development, twists and suspense whilst seeing if we could not disappoint the main audience.

As a filmmaker do you have to accept that film is a business, whereby you are required to compromise the business with the art?

It is definitely the case that in the end it is a product, although it would be different if I were making films in Germany where it is pure art, and it is financed through the government. But here you have to be aware that people are investing a lot of money. **THE LAST EXORCISM**, for example, cost *only* $1.5 million to make, but then they invested $24 million in marketing. So there is some serious money and risk involved for someone. You want to make the best film possible, but you also want the world to see it, which means you have to juggle the expectations of film as a product, and you have to feed your artistic integrity—you have to find the balance within that.

I don't care about gore, and I don't get a kick out of blood. I remember after **THE LAST EXORCISM** our actress [Ashley Bell] did an interview with a horror magazine over here, and the first question they asked her was whether there was a blood pump on set when we were shooting. Did you use a blood pump? That to them was the criteria of whether it was a good movie or not. I never necessarily cared about the amount of gore, but I don't mind it either. So if I am making a movie for Dimension then you can do that scene bloodless like we did with **THE LAST EXORCISM** where there was hardly a drop of blood or with a bucket of blood. It doesn't make a difference to me narratively in the scene, but that's the moment that I can think about how they are going to market it—who is my producer and investor, and then I can try to give them what they obviously hired me for.

Filmmakers have frequently spoken to me about how they direct whilst they write. How do the two inform one another for you personally?

Well, I always get heavily involved in the development of a project. The main writer of **THE LAST EXORCISM**, David Birke, who co-wrote **13 SINS**, was never credited. We sat together for months and wrote it, and the way we worked was he would write something, give it to me and I would send him notes. Sometimes it would be more pages than what he actually wrote. Then we would go back and forth, and so it ends up in the territory where he is co-writing, which actually works really well because when I was a writer I found the loneliness of it all terrifying.

If you make a mistake in the first act then the chances are you are not going to realize it until two or three months later, when you are in the third act and you realize you have gone down the wrong path and lost three months of your life. If you are working with someone then that is not a problem, because you have someone you can bounce ideas off. Therefore it will probably take an afternoon for you to figure out that it's the wrong way to go. That is the great luxury to me in directing because you are never alone, and there is always someone who you are talking to or communicating with who is a specialist in their field. At first it is the writer, and then it is the actors, cinematographer, production designer and editor. There is always someone you can turn to and say, "This is what I have in mind, what do you think?" You can always check every idea every step of the way, which can sometimes be infuriating if you are trying to get an idea through, and there is somebody who says, "This just doesn't make sense." But in the end you are glad to have that, because by the time it reaches the audience it has been checked so many times that the main parts of the idea that you are trying to communicate hopefully makes sense. Whereas if I was a completely independent writer and director who didn't have anybody to check ideas at every corner then the risk is obviously much bigger.

I know that a lot of directors dread the test screening process, and it is terrifying because you have a raw version of your movie—a cut that isn't complete yet, which you are presenting to a random group of people that will inevitably tear it apart. They will just sink their teeth into it because it doesn't have the music or sound design, and it's not colour corrected. Everything that makes it look glossy, professional and makes people forgive the mistakes is not done yet, and so it's like this vulnerable thing that doesn't have any armour. But it is so important, because if your movie doesn't survive those first test screenings or if you don't have time to react to those results and to edit accordingly; to then check with a group of people their emotions towards the film who are not attached to it, then that step will happen once it is released. At that point you can't do anything about it, and so it is a vital step.

From the beginning it is not about blood or gore, it is not about horror but first and foremost it is about the characters and how the circumstances manipulate them into their choices. Your thoughts on how you use characters, because you use them with passion and love.

I think the trick in order for horror to work is that you have to care about the characters. That's nothing new—they are not words of wisdom. But I think the

Ashley Bell goes all to Hell as Nell Sweetzer in **THE LAST EXORCISM**

Mark Webber draws a bead in **13 SINS**

first third if not the first half of the movie to a certain degree should be spent making sure the audience falls in love with the characters. One big weapon we used to achieve this in **THE LAST EXORCISM** was humour. Just because it is a genre or a horror movie doesn't mean it should be doom or gloom from the first to the last minute. You need to have moments that the audience can spend with the protagonists and enjoy and get a kick out of. In **THE LAST EXORCISM** we used a lot of humour in the first half, and then completely faded it out so that you will not find a single upbeat moment in the second half of the movie. In the first half it's full of humour because it's all about the bonding between the audience and the characters to ensure the audience both like the characters and want to see them succeed. Then you have the audience by the throat because you can do things to the characters/protagonists that are horrific, and the audience will suffer with them. All the horror in the world is not horrific if you don't care about the person that it is happening to, and with **13 SINS** we tried to find some humour in the absurdity of everything, but also to spend as much time as possible trying to make the audience identify with the character.

It is hard because you have to find the line where you are telling the story of a pushover and a weakling without the audience running out of patience for the character. It is a fine line between saying, "Oh he can't defend himself or stand up for himself, poor guy…I like him" to "I don't want to be with that guy because he should grow a pair of balls, and I'm not going to sit here and follow his journey." Then it became about how much pressure do we put on this character so that he can start to do these horrific things, yet we still understand why he does it, whilst ensuring we don't judge him for it.

We did a first draft in which the only reason he did it was for the money—there was no father that was going to move in and there was no brother that was going to be institutionalized. Instead there was just this guy who doesn't have a lot of money, and when he's offered this large sum he just takes it, which I think in real life for most people would be understandable, although it would be morally questionable, which is what is so interesting about it. If someone offered me $6 million to forget my morals for a day then I think I might be tempted. But then other people like Bob Weinstein who is a billionaire obviously doesn't understand that, and so he said, "Oh well that doesn't make any sense. He needs to be more likable." So then we started throwing in all this other stuff—the debt from the student loan, his father who is going to move in, his pregnant fiancée etc. It is almost ridiculous how much financial pressure this guy is under, but we were just trying to hit that point where everyone would understand why he does it, which of course you could argue is also what makes it a little less interesting as it's not about the character.

My argument when discussing it with Bob Weinstein was that if you push it to the point where everyone would do it—where you or I would do it, and where to do it is the only ethically moral choice then it becomes a lot less interesting. What we do is whitewash this character to a degree that he isn't a character anymore, but rather just a stand in for every one of us. Looking back at it now that was maybe exactly the point of trying to create an everyman character that is just a stand-in for the audience—someone who you, me and everyone can surrender to the characteristics of.

Reading a review of CHEAP THRILLS it was argued that giving the character no choice would have made for a better film. How important is it to give characters a choice and not to back them into a corner? Surely allowing a character free will make for a more interesting commentary on morality?

I haven't seen **CHEAP THRILLS** but I hear it's great, and in every review someone mentions it. But I agree with you that the character needs to have free will. We had that argument where Weinstein said, "Why don't we have the game kidnap his fiancée, put a gun to her head and say, 'If you don't do these things we'll kill her.'" I said, "Well that's not a movie I'd be remotely interested in making because how is that interesting—everyone would do it." If you kidnapped my girlfriend and put a gun to her head I would do anything because there is no longer a choice.

All great drama is about choices, and 99% is about best intentions, but then especially in tragedies it goes horribly wrong. But we do need to allow our characters to make that choice, and we must count on the audience to understand that kind of struggle. If you have people that have such a moral high ground that they say with genuine conviction "I would never do that", then we have lost them in the beginning, and I am not making movies for those people. I think you have to understand and have a feeling for that little bit of darkness yourself that then makes all these things horrific, because it is potentially possible.

You have spoken about not wanting to be solely associated with horror. With the ability to write, does that help alleviate some of the pressure, and help open up new avenues for you or is still a difficult situation to tell a story you want to tell outside of being pigeonholed as a horror director?

The reality of it all is if you start a project from scratch and you sit down to write a script today, then it is probably going to be ten years before you get to make that movie. You have to find people who are willing to finance it. I have so many friends who go down that avenue and the financing goes away. Then they try to fund raise and everyone wants to change it, and it ends up being a huge process that wouldn't allow you to pay the rent—that's the problem.

If you want to be a professional filmmaker I think the other thing you have to juggle and you touched on a little bit earlier is the economics of it all. You have to find projects that are already green lit that you can take on and develop further. If you start from scratch it is just going to take too long. If I want to pay rent I need to make a movie every two years, and in order to do that I have to find something that is already out there. This is limiting not because there is so little out there, but in my career right now great scripts are going to bigger people—they are going to the Finchers or whoever are out there. What trickles down to me is not necessarily great material, and so what I have to do is find a project that has a really interesting core to it—some idea that I can develop. It doesn't have to be a brilliant script that comes to me as-is, but at the same time I don't want to do horror again and again and again. I'm really comfortable in the dark thriller corner but in the end I'll do anything if it is a great story. I'll do a Western or a sci-fi if it's a great story—I just need something.

I had an epiphany recently when I was standing at the traffic lights and I thought, I hope Jenny is okay. Then I thought who's Jenny—I don't know a Jenny. I realised Jenny was a character from a script I had read two or three weeks ago. I couldn't remember the story, the genre but I knew that I cared about this Jenny character. In a story a character can live on in your head for a couple of weeks after, and that is kind of what I'm looking for, but it is so hard to find and it is rare. It is a tough job, but the toughest job is not making the movie but rather finding the material for the movie that you want to make.

Weng's Chop *Magazine would like to thank Art and Daniel for the fantastic interview! To follow Daniel online, check him out at* twitter.com/StammDaniel

Ron Perlman in Stamm's **13 SINS** (2014)

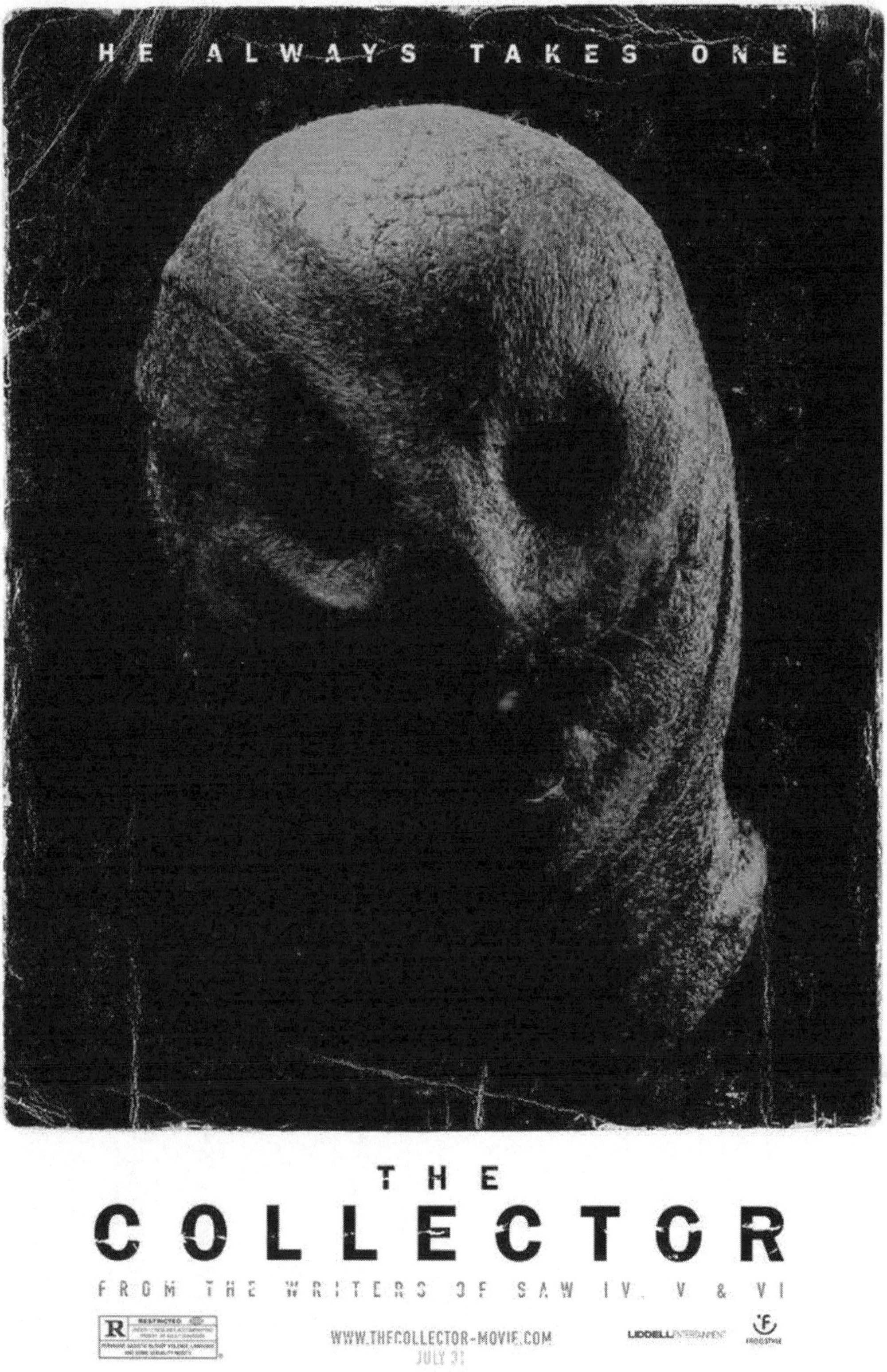

HE ALWAYS TAKES ONE

THE COLLECTOR

FROM THE WRITERS OF SAW IV, V & VI

 WWW.THECOLLECTOR-MOVIE.COM
JULY 31

A COLLECTION OF THOUGHT:
AN INTERVIEW WITH MARCUS DUNSTAN

by Art Stevenson

Weng's Chop *magazine recently had the privilege to get into the mind of one of the architects of the* Saw *franchise, the writer/director of the provocative home invasion and labyrinth puzzle box films* **THE COLLECTOR** *(2009) and* **THE COLLECTION** *(2012), Marcus Dunstan. In what was an honest conversation full of humour, Marcus shared with us the influence of Tom Savini that led to a contemplation of Romero's enduring zombie classics, creating a complex narrative web, working with Josh Stewart and how Arkin's origins emerged out of a filmic concept, and he also offered us an insight into what* **THE COLLECTION** *and* **THE COLLECTOR** *might have been under different circumstances.*

Why a career in filmmaking? Was there that one inspirational moment?

It was learning about Tom Savini's craft, and how he evolved from a love of magic to photography. From his experiences of the Vietnam War through a camera, and the way that he gave to his country in that way, to coming back home to create a movie experience for people that could still keep a wall of fantasy up between us, and the real terrors that were out there. He did so with a sleight of hand. It was with a camera that wouldn't have to look away or cut anymore, and he could bridge the gap between the impossible, and the shocking.

Then all of a sudden Mr. Savini was in front of the camera as Blades in **DAWN OF THE DEAD** (1978), and wait didn't he also do a stunt? Oh my gosh, it looks like he was playing multiple characters—doing makeup effects and playing a role. I saw this gentleman become a jack of all trades, and he was very giving of the knowledge as well as those who had inspired him in his wonderful book, *Grande Illusions*. So he shared his knowledge with people like me who were trying to get a grip on why I was so terribly scared by movies, but also why I loved them.

I was dissecting the special effects and understanding the magic of it. Of course you are seeing something that is absolutely real, and yet something that isn't real. At that point I was dissecting my own fear mechanism, and I wanted to contribute and make something that would scare someone else.

So in 1990 when **NIGHT OF THE LIVING DEAD** came out, there was Tom Savini the director. The gentleman who had inspired, shared and created was now telling a story with all those components already under his belt. The gentleman who knew how to build a ship was now a captain.

Tom Savini in **DAWN OF THE DEAD**, with beverage of choice

What is it that makes NIGHT OF THE LIVING DEAD (1968) such an enduring film?

I believe one of Wes Craven's favourite films is the original **NIGHT OF THE LIVING DEAD**, and it was the movie MTV would play on Halloween in the 'Eighties. I'm guessing but it was because Mr Romero didn't just make a film that existed for those moments of shock value between the screams. He started out with a social allegory that was enhanced by something or someone in the form of the living dead that would throttle and bite you.

The original **DAWN OF THE DEAD**, I more often than not listen to the first fifteen to twenty minutes of it over and over again. It has such a marvellous sound design; where you are just listening to a news station

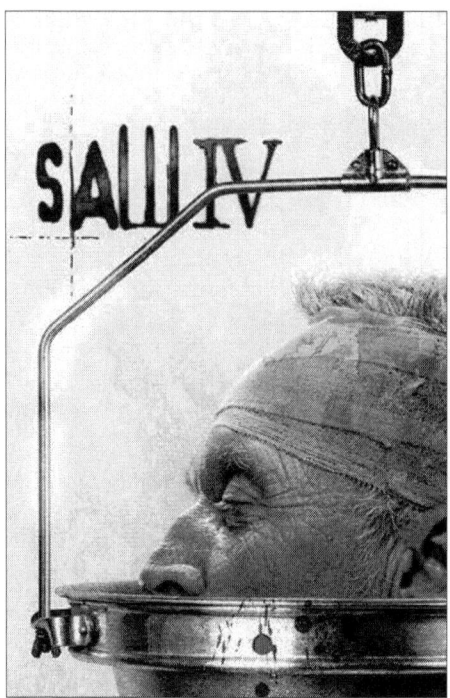

lose control on information. We are listening to a society lose its hope. It didn't require 100 million dollars. It didn't require massive cityscape shots. It was a tiny broadcast station in Pittsburgh, and yet they were the last stand for people who needed to seek shelter, needed clear information, and needed help because everything was on fire. The general flow of information is so tactfully done, and you have the strumming Goblin score comprised of just a pulse that seems to be keeping steady amongst a world gone erratic. It's marvellous filmmaking and storytelling, and it is a social allegory. In the first five or ten minutes we haven't even seen a zombie yet. It is just watching people react to something that they can no longer control.

What were the events that led to your involvement in SAW IV (2007)?

We were brought into a room to watch an early assembly of **SAW III** (2006). We were tasked with coming up with an idea for **SAW IV**, as we're two other writers. It was a contest situation, which wasn't anything new to Patrick or me, as we had just completed one with *Project Greenlight* (2001-2002). Only this time we were up against three people rather than twelve hundred. Despite this smaller number, it did not feel that the odds were any more in our favour. In fact we were the only team who didn't get the Bible that outlined what the rules were for the *Saw* movies. We only had what was in our heads. But it was awesome because the on-paper disadvantage turned out to be an advantage, primarily because we didn't want to betray the creativity that was going on with those first three films. They felt rather complete—they told a story that was enhancing and growing. **SAW IV** had every possibility of just being another one, but we were allowed to push and create some moments that honoured the fact that it was a sequel, that took advantage of the fact that there was a history, and yet pushed to expand that. So it felt like it needed to exist, and it deserved to exist to honour the marvellous work that had come before it.

From the **Feast** *trilogy to the* **Saw** *franchise, you have confronted the horror sequel and furthermore the horror franchise. They are both intertwined with the story of the horror genre. How challenging does it become as the films roll on by?*

It is all dependent on the stimulus. You can make a sequel where all you do is repeat the first movie, and where you just add more blood. That goes back to **JAWS 2** (1978), which is a pretty fun movie. By that point where could **JAWS** (1975) go? Whilst the first movie could take advantage of not having seen the shark yet, in the second movie we have already seen it. So we have to see it again, but this time bigger than before, which creates a "more" effect. By the time you get to **JAWS 3D** (1983) they are just throwing 3D at the problem [laughs]. With Jaws 4 what is going on? Boy oh boy. Yet I tell you I would be in that opening night line if they were to remake **JAWS** and take it back to the shadows.

So sequels—is there more of a story to tell? Well of course, because the right creative brain can always come up with a great story—**ALIENS** (1986), **THE EMPIRE STRIKES BACK** (1980), and **STAR TREK II: THE WRATH OF KHAN** (1982). There are stories that take advantage of the fact that they are a continuing chapter.

I saw **ALIENS** first. I didn't even know there was a movie called **ALIEN** (1979). I was up late watching HBO one night and Aliens just happened to be on. It was about this woman who had been through something and she just happened to know a little about a planet that might be overrun with something really bad. So when I finally saw **ALIEN** it was an origin story, and all it was about for me was creating Ripley's fear, and introducing the story behind her relationship with this predator. **ALIENS** is still a marvellous movie in its own right, and it stands on its own legs. It is war and it is just marvellous.

I saw **THE EMPIRE STRIKES BACK** when I was so young that I didn't have a concept of a sequel. It was just a continuation; just more of the story, and what a marvellous story. It is one that got into my heart and I remember feeling bad when they hurt Han. I wanted it to be okay when Leah said, "I love you." But then oh my gosh, there's a twist at the end. It was great.

With **STAR TREK II** I didn't have the twenty-five years of television history. I had never seen an episode of the *Star Trek* TV show, but Ricardo Montalban's burnt face yelling at William Shatner over his dying friend…I was galvanised. I actually remember falling asleep during the first **STAR TREK** (1979) movie.

The **Saw** *franchise resembles a complex web, and a friend once told me that during a writing class he unsuccessfully attempted to map out the Saw narrative on a sheet of A4 paper.*

[Laughs] We did the same thing. I had a wall in my apartment and I painted it red. But it took five or six coats until it was red enough to be the think wall for **SAW IV**. Patrick and I filled out so many index cards with ideas that it looked like we'd shingled the house. Then we had these huge three-foot by four-foot Post-it's where we were making timelines, and character lines. We had that dissected down to the skin pore. It was a way to find out which circles had closed, which ones could still be open, and which ones we could tweak.

James Wan is a master of employing image and sound to turn his audience's imagination against them, to use it as a stimulus for suspense and terror. How important and influential is Wan in modern horror?

I wouldn't be a part of this interview if it wasn't for James Wan. He inspires. He and Leigh Whannell as a partnership have created horror that grabs the teen and the child in equal measure. They have marvellously kept the story in mind; not just the scares. I have seen **THE CONJURING** (2013) now five times, and I love it because it is not a horror movie for the sake of being a horror movie. It really takes these characters we care for, and yes it puts them through the wringer, but it develops them. We care for them, and when Vera Farmiga looks at Patrick Wilson and says, "We are here for a reason and this is it" then your bones turn to steel. We want them to beat on evil, even though it might cost them everything. That singular moment is a marvellous touchstone for where horror can go.

There is the old adage "You have to go through Hell to get to Heaven." Horror filmmakers have a cruel streak that sometimes ignores the conclusion of this journey towards paradise, but is one that perhaps owes a lot to CARRIE's (1976) influential final scare.

Well, to a light-hearted degree that's where we get **EVIL DEAD 2** (1987) and **ARMY OF DARKNESS** (1992). Not the remake which was more of the former. The original **THE EVIL DEAD** (1981) was a savage and cruel exercise in terror. Personally I want our hero to ask for it and then get it. I don't like the idea of someone who is well intentioned and it resulting in savage cruelty.

It's hard because I am a hypocrite in that I did do that for sure in a couple of stories. I took an innocent, I throttled them and I hurt them terribly. Upon watching it and it settling with me for a couple of years, those are the images that are hard to watch. With the character of Arkin in **THE COLLECTOR** for example, I am punishing a thief in a *Twilight Zone*-mixed-with-terror sort of way.

Left to right: Marcus Dunstan & Patrick Melton

What I like about Arkin's actions in **THE COLLECTION** is that he's a guy who is fortified by that experience. Life is going to throw you or anyone challenges, and often in the horror movie they are to balance out a terrible day. This is in the sense that no matter how rough your day was, how bad traffic was or if the job was taken away from you; no matter if you even got shoved into a locker, the horror movie is not only there to show you someone having an even worse day, but showing you someone you can identify with or look up to in order to survive and tower above it. With the character of Arkin I wanted some of that. I wanted someone who had been through so much that there is not one psycho, bully or act of God that can hurt him more than he is willing to hurt himself to hit 'em back.

Josh Stewart possesses a powerful onscreen presence, allowing him even in THE DARK KNIGHT RISES *(2012) to divert your gaze from the lead actors in a scene. How do you look back on the opportunity to collaborate with Josh across* THE COLLECTOR *and* THE COLLECTION?

A gift to any film is an actor who respects it, and Josh is that actor. He's been a marvellous friend to me, and he's been a marvellous friend to anyone who has been lucky enough to get to know him. Being side-by-side with him, and facing the gauntlet that we did on those two films, it was my privilege to be in his company. He showed such a generosity from his end through a performance that is just pitch perfect.

I'm thrilled because I now have a friend who's also a tremendous actor. I knew he would get it in the first take, but I would shoot two takes regardless in case the first one wasn't in focus. But I had that one in the arsenal all of the time. He just had it; he just showed up. There was the character, what have you got? That allowed us to push and to exploit the scenes, because we could maximise the time we had to shoot by not having to go on a journey of discovery for every line and scene. He was just on it. It felt like I could almost bring a documentary approach to his acting. I could plant the camera anywhere and he was there. He was great.

We get him on the big screen next month in **TRANSCENDENCE** (2014). Oh, and here's another aspect—he's a director now, too. His film is called **THE HUNTED** (2013), and I have had the privilege of seeing it two and a half times now. I saw it in the rough, which was a half viewing, and then I have seen the completed cut twice now. It is awesome and once again he brings the greatest resources he can. He's the writer, director and star, and he handles every single position with marvellous control and authority.

In THE COLLECTOR *the journey of Stewart's Arkin character is one that transitions from villain to hero, even one might say an unlikely hero.*

Well the goal of **THE COLLECTOR** was what if the character Alan Arkin played in **WAIT UNTIL DARK** (1967) was the hero, hence his name is Arkin. What if James Caan from Michael Mann's **THIEF** (1981) ran afoul of The Tooth Fairy from **MANHUNTER** (1986)? Well that sounded like a fun concept or scenario. If you take a villain from a thriller and put him up against the villain of a horror movie, your villain from a thriller is all of a sudden not so bad. That alchemy was very exciting from a storytelling point of view, but also from the point of view of a movie. Our thoughts of the movies out there were, okay we can see the latest lovely woman who can really fill out a dirty wet tank top, can fight another lumbering, not-too-eloquent beast with a weapon of choice. It was far more challenging to say I want to take a broken father and I want to use all the sharp edges of his soul to turn him into one last weapon to take down this devil. Along the way, sure, there is a lovely woman who is in a form-fitting tank top [laughs].

When working on the first film did you intend for there to be a sequel?

We knew we had an opportunity to create a horror villain that could ask for another film, and one that could potentially create questions. But our goal was to create a lead character and to complete a story. What inspired the sequel more than anything was not only the opportunity—it was really the company saying "Hey we made enough money to try another one." But intrinsically that's one moment. That maybe gets the cheque written; that gets the contract. It does not inspire a creative ounce. That still has to come from a personal place unless you just want to write off two years of your life, and not give a rip about what comes out.

There was one comment that inspired the film. It was during a test screening of the original **COLLECTOR**. There was a woman who sat in the audience. Now we get all the cards back and we obsessively read every single one of them. The people by and large were all very concise, though this one woman wrote in very plain text, "The ending left me with no hope." That hurt. I knew that was what we had done, and I had intended to do that. I actually went out of pocket and shot that ending myself—alone. So I knew I took away the broken father. I knew I'd shoved him in a box. I knew I'd let the bad guy win. That line right there was a case of "you're right, thank you". Now I know what the sequel will be. It was then that I knew it was going to be about that broken father getting out and learning to stand on a bully's neck.

You can turn the dialogue off on **THE COLLECTION**. Each movie had a wild art-house approach in the beginning. My blue sky scenario when I was writing **THE COLLECTOR** was that I wanted to shoot it in black and white anamorphic with James Franco reprising his role as James Dean. It was going to be the lost James Dean movie that he did, but it was just too violent to come out at the time. It would look like a 'Fifties era movie.

My art-house idea for the second one which got me through it was the idea of having no dialogue. In fact I made it in Italian and I lost all the sound. It had to be recomposed with score in the visual because its simple themes were so apparent. But the survivor isn't willing to be a victim anymore. There is that one nagging responsibility to protect life, which is born in him and comes to completion when in the end he is willing to give it all away to save the one he left be-

hind. You know what—he actually found somebody who he did save, and who had the mechanism already, and was willing to run back into the fire and save the broken man.

Weng's Chop *magazine would like to thank Art and Marcus for the fantastic interview and wealth of information and insight. To find out more about Marcus Dunstan and his work, follow him at* twitter.com/MarcusDunstan

ARTICLES

ADVENTURES IN PORNO LAND

by Louis Paul

I've decided to review new and recent DVD releases from Vinegar Syndrome for a number of reasons. Mostly, because they take me back to a time when these films, or those similar were just the right kind of thing for someone into the cinema of transgression.

I started haunting Times Square at an early age. I frequented the theaters on 42nd Street showing double- (and in some cases, triple-) bills. There was a theater, The Victory on the north end of 7th Avenue and Broadway that was a porn theater. One day I got up the nerve, walked up to the (curtained...I guess so you couldn't see anyone in the booth) box-office plunked down my $2.75 and walked in. I still remember the movies—**THE LIFE AND TIMES OF THE HAPPY HOOKER** *(1974)* with Samantha McLaren, double-billed with **ORIENTAL ECSTASY GIRLS** *(1974)*. Even more than seeing John Homes' huge dick on this big screen, I recall how dark it was in the theater... real freakin' dark. Remembering all this, I recall the strange smell as well. A mix of cigarettes (back in those days you could still smoke in New York movie theaters) and something else. That something else probably was accumulated cum spewed out onto the floor, into handkerchiefs, mouths...whatever.

I recall barely able to discern where the seating area began and the aisles ended. I think I stood frozen for a few seconds (that felt like minutes) watching a giant pussy get banged in color on a huge screen...and hearing "ohhhh" and "ahhhh" echoing throughout what seemed like a cavernous room.

I think I watched **ECSTASY GIRLS** twice before I walked out into the night. Suddenly I had this fear that someone I knew would see me walking out of a porn theater so I took a quick swerve onto Broadway and walking fast walked two blocks out of my way to the train.

Afterwards, I started going to the Times Square area and 42nd street for my "education". Back in those days, the movies on 42nd St. changed at least twice a week. So, in one week you could see a ton of stuff.

I consider the pornographic films made from 1972-1985 among the best movies that the adult cinema could provide. These films contained for the most part, stories, sometimes good ones. The actresses were hot, and even when they weren't they made up for that with enthusiasm. And yes, the majority of the films were arousing. Even bold, notorious movies like **CANDY STRIPERS** (1978) and **BABYFACE** (1977), the sort of films you shouldn't be finding entertaining, much less arousing, were due to an oddly hypnotic combination of story and enthusiastic performances.

After this prime period, filmmakers learned it was cheaper to shoot on video, and only a small handful of titles, usually those by Michael Ninn (**SHOCK** [1996], **LATEX** [1995]), who happened to be a favorite of, of all people, Jess Franco, entertained. When pornography moved into everyone's home via the Internet, everything changed. The feeling of transgression became absent. It's all another "click a link" and "next". Sometimes, you find gold, like some old film that I saw playing on 42nd St. but the print is washed out and battered, uploaded by some private collector from a dusted off old VHS tape or in some cases, a ratty 16mm print.

Which brings me to the reason why I love the guys at Vinegar Syndrome, and the restoration work they are doing on adult films from the past. In most cases, they have taken the original negatives, or as close to that source as they can get, and remastered the source material for today's audiences obsessed with digital restoration.

DEEP ROOTS
1978, USA. D: Joseph Bardo (as Lisa Barr)
S: *Jesse Chacan, Anita Sands, Mari Swan, Liz Renay, Toni Bell, Debbie Love*

Billy (Jesse Chacan) leaves the American Indian reservation where he's been raised and hops on his motorcycle and decides to see what the tail end of the hedonistic 'Seventies can offer him on the west coast. Billy strolls down Hollywood Boulevard accompanied by groovy sounds and as he ponders his skills as a modernist painter, in minutes he finds his first model (Sands) who takes him back to her place, disrobes and disorients our star Rembrandt by giving him a tasty blowjob. After a rather dull fuck session, Billy disappears to have sex with another woman he finds attractive (Bell), but after a while throws her friend on the back of his cycle instead and off they ride to semen nirvana.

For some reason, too much of the screen time of this 76 minute feature is now suddenly devoted to former Andy Warhol confidant Liz Renay who performs an awkward striptease and lounges around reading her autobiography while another chick (Love) gets the full hairstylist treatment—hairy bush trimming included. Liz is prepping the marriage of the first woman Billy met while in LA (Sands).

When Billy finally turns up again, there's a swingers' party in progress, and a man dressed as Groucho Marx (full make-up and wisecracks included). Is this all too much for Billy? Will he finally get to bed Toni Bell? Will he run away from all the hot girls lusting for his sun-drenched loins and return home?

I have to give a round of applause to the mighty blue archivists at Vinegar Syndrome for unearthing this title that I've never ever heard of, much less a mighty contribution to the fetish genre charitably called "hairy pussies". The film will blow you away with its clarity, wild 'Seventies colors, comfortable southern California style 'Seventies rock...and lots and lots of hairy bush. As far as acting skills are concerned, star Chacan (an actual American Indian) is decent enough, and is handsome as well. The remainder of the cast is forgettable, and while certainly not wastrel junkie types, they can't act and only Anita Sands seems skillful during her energetic sex scenes. Liz Renay's presence in this film might be a mystery (former stripper, girlfriend of notorious gangsters, actress in Ed Wood, Arch Hall, and John Waters films and hanger-on at Andy Warhol's Factory) if she didn't also appear in a few Ray Dennis Steckler flicks, too. Director Bardo was a friend of Steckler's who assisted on some of his low low low budget films, including **THE THRILL KILLERS** (1964) where Renay had a role. Still the print is amazing and worth the fun. Hell, you might even return to this title now and again for purely historical reasons.

STARLET NIGHTS
1978, USA. D: Joseph Bardo (as Lisa Barr)
S: *Leslie Bovee, Candy Nichols, Kandi Barbour, Tyler Reynolds, Jesse Chacan, Rick Roberts*

Remember the fairy tale of Snow White? Well, this is one of the earliest XXX versions of that tale. Leslie Bovee wakes in bed and in an incredibly randy mood, rubs her hands all over her very hairy pussy and implores the magical fey genie (Tyler Horne) in the mirror *"Who is the most beautiful woman alive?"* expecting to hear that it's her. Instead the pissed off genie claims it is the young virginal stepdaughter Snow (Candy Nichols) who is the fairest one of them all.

Bovee then demands that the magic mirror provide a well-hung stud or two to satisfy the uncontrolled lust building between her moist hot thighs. After a few costumed goons appear out of nowhere and have sex with her (including Jesse Chacan who had a much larger role in **DEEP ROOTS**) because she claims her husband cannot take care of her needs, Bovee takes to a large cucumber as well...and well...you get the idea. Much of the 81-minute running time is devoted to the wicked stepmother's plan involving the virginal Snow, who must partake of a bite of the horny apple and lose her virginity. As we reach the climax, like **DEEP ROOTS**, there's another costume party orgy, and most of the cast get to go home happy.

Remastered from the original negative, despite **STARLET NIGHTS'** brevity of plot it just looks spectacular thanks to the restoration from VS. The

vivid colors pop out from the screen like never before and if anyone wanted to see star Bovee's flappy labia up close and moist, this is the place to come to. On its own, this is an occasionally enjoyable comedy-porn film, but this type of story was done so much better elsewhere (see **7 INTO SNOWY** [1978]), and no one else besides Bovee is very memorable, not even Jesse Chacan in a small role as man meat wearing a ridiculous costume. After showing much promise in **DEEP ROOTS** (for the same director), he's all but thrust into the background here.

MARILYN AND THE SENATOR
1975, USA. D: Carlos Tobalina
S: Nina Fause, William Margold, Heather Leigh, Sharon Thorpe, Liz Renay

If there was an altar of sleaze, I think fans of '70s era smut would be lined up around the block to kneel before the video conservationists who run Vinegar Syndrome. Even I am mighty impressed when they unload a pristine remastered print of another novel title that I have never heard of, and it turns out to be an epic length (over two hours!) comedy/political caper/sex movie!

Marilyn (Fause) stars as Marilyn, a woman who appears at the Washington, DC office of nebbish slob U.S. senator William Margold. She explains that she's a close friend of one of his hookers (he has an apartment reserved for such sexual encounters at the Watergate Hotel), and that said person has told her about his being hung, and his sexual proclivities. As the Senator explains he's married, Marilyn just blows this off. She wants his child. Rather…she wants him to fuck her on a regular basis…and because he's smart (I don't think so), etc., she believes him to be a good candidate for the…position. However, once they finally get together to do just that (as Queep, the Senator's secretary spies on them in the process via an archaic spy cam…while masturbating), the politician just can't get it up enough to perform.

For some reason, Marilyn telephones the local madam (faded whiz post Liz Renay) and tells her she seeks a John for the evening because she's too turned on and needs a release. The guy Liza sends her to is a Zen master of fucking…and wants to do mystical things before they join together…but Marilyn will have none of this. She just wants to get laid by a pro…and does.

Meanwhile, the Senator's wife happens by the office as he's getting serviced by one of his hooker girlfriends in the hotel and catches Queep in mid-jizz explosion as he's watching everything on the spy cam. Suddenly, the Senator's wife thinks of hatching her own plan once Queep tells her of Marilyn's scheme.

Bill Margold is a natural at comedy, and his bedroom exploit scenes have a touch of real life naiveté. Nina Fause, however, in what I understand is one of only two or three X-rated titles she ever appeared in, is as stiff as a board. While she's certainly a looker…she's not stunning. Her facial expressions ranging from doe-eyed deer being hypnotized to doe-eyed deer being hypnotized. Yes, she's got one facial expression and that's it for the entire running time. She's not much more energetic in bed either. In a way, I can see why Margold's Senator has a tough time getting it up when she's just okay at what is supposed to be her line of work. Thank goodness that other actresses are around like Sharon Thorpe who at the least makes some of the sex scenes more tolerable considering that director Tobalina shot them for long takes.

Speaking of the director, one of the disc's many extras is an astounding audio commentary where much discussion is given to his work methods, and directing techniques (he was apparently something of an experimenter within the hardcore genre with both subject matter, and the length of the films). Bill Margold is on-hand with others and you'll hear often hysterical accounts of the making of **MARILYN AND THE SENATOR** and hear Margold refer to leading lady Fause as having acting ability below that of a corpse (ouch!). I highly recommend this release (a standalone disc) for it being an absolutely bonkers curio. Maybe not so much as titillation for the raincoat crowd (hey, you're home now…sitting on the couch…so I guess anything goes).

THE VIXENS OF KUNG FU: A TALE OF YIN YANG
1975, USA. D: Bill Milling
S: Bree Anthony, Tony Richards, Peonies Jong, C.J. Laing, Jamie Gillis, Roger Caine, Bobby Astyr

This stunning (not in a good way) oddball film is so bizarre in nearly every way…my brain hurts just attempting to find the correct words to describe it.

In a small conclave in the woods, a community of female Zen-like worshipers sits in a circle. Since they are all wearing lightly colored gowns and robes with cleavage showing, we know that we've come to the right place to see **THE VIXENS OF KUNG FU**. As a master practitioner performs some awkwardly choreographed flailing arms version of what somebody thought practicing kung fu might be like, the girls all sit around, lick their lips…and before you can say "blowjob scene", just that happens. Apparently all these girls (led by C.J. Laing) worship some sort of mystical deity of sex and martial arts. Since both are awkwardly portrayed, I was thinking maybe it was a mystical lesbian cult at first. Later when a mystical ninja monk who has been tracking this group for a long time (don't ask) finds them and spends a good deal of his time exercising his schlong with the various members…well, I realized anything goes in this epic of nonsense. Then, suddenly out of nowhere we follow Bree Anthony as she apparently is walking through one of the more deserted areas of Central Park when suddenly she is set upon by three crazed sex fiends (Gillis and Astyr among them). She is shot in the ass with what looks like a dart gun, and in a fleeting moment of directorial whimsy, our three Caucasian thugs carefully place a picnic blanket on the ground before violating her. But she appears to not be entirely under the influence of the dart gun drug as her blow jobs are quite enthusiastic.

Next scene, we appear to be involved in more goofy initiations before a wayward male martial artist-in-training appears at a diner and meets Peonies Jung, the first true Asian we've seen in this film so far. Just as we think a sex scene may happen with these two… the woman who was molested in the park appears and while she seems to still be drugged, Sapphic rituals bring her back to herself and cue flashbacks to sex scenes (including a brief rehash of the park assault).

In truth there is more girl-on-girl action in the film than hetero, but that's not always a bad thing, just that few of the performers appear to be enthusiastic about their roles (aside from Bree Anthony, who gets to reprise one of the movie's hotter moments).

As the film ends, rather abruptly, you'll most likely remember that odd scene and have a few questions yourself, like why does one of the trio of male rapists refuse to partake in the orgy and instead masturbate

on the woman's colorful socks? Why when all the women get mystically turned on with their amateurish workout does smoke emanate from their privates (not special FX stuff, but rather someone off-screen blowing cigarettes smoke from between their legs), and why does the movie blow the one opportunity to showcase the one lone obviously Asian female in the cast to have an inhibited sex scene?

Another oddball touch is that director Milling (who helmed the popular VHS sexploitation rental **CAGED FURY** (1990) among other titles in later years) chose to people his film with a cast of performers and crew with mainly pseudonymous names ("Lin Chen Fiu", "Ling Fat", etc.) and much of the film was post-synched with an odd delay like much of the 42nd street Hong Kong titles back in the day. Possibly it was a ruse to trick exhibitors into thinking this was either an actual sexy martial arts flick from HK or worse… an actual kung fu flick that could mistakenly be programmed next to **5 FINGERS OF DEATH** (1972) or **BRUCE LEE FIGHTS BACK FROM THE GRAVE** (1976).

ORIENTAL BLUE
1975, USA. D: Bill Milling
S: Peonies Jong, Kim Pope. Bree Anthony, Terri Hall, C.J. Laing, Bobby Astyr, Jamie Gillis, Alan Marlow, Ashley Moore

Decidedly sleazier and scuzzier than **VIXENS OF KUNG FU** (which is on the same disc as this film), **ORIENTAL BLUE** is the one you all came to read

about. Madame Blue (Jong) runs a sex trafficking business and her hideout is located in New York's Chinatown area. Her clients include foreign dignitaries, the wealthy, and spies both foreign and domestic. The middle-aged Madame Blue assigns her personal male assistants to wander the Broadway theater district, interest women, bring them back and then drug them with a serum that turns them into wanton sex freaks. With the potential to go really dark here with the subject matter, it's all thankfully relatively restrained.

The amount of sexual sizzle on display here is of a high degree, with some of the scenes running to near-real-time. With each kidnapping, drugging, and seduction the film tilts ever more into its own kind of hysteria. I kept hoping that the exotic Madame Blue would participate in something.

It's not long before she does, and well…she's quite adept at eating bush (possibly a preference for the actress?) especially that of Terri Hall, who plays her own personal assistant, and, it appears, sex slave as well. The Madame also indulges in a few threesomes as well, some of them deliriously steamy.

Peonies Jung (obviously not her real name) only appeared in three other films (besides a small part in **VIXENS OF KUNG FU**), **WHEN A WOMAN CALLS** (1975) and **BLOWDRY** (1976) and four loops.

A mature woman when she appeared in this movie, she appeared older than other (and far more popular) hardcore starlet Linda Wong, and in all likelihood was hovering somewhere in her mid-thirties to early forties but turns in a decent performance as the in-sidious sex slaver and is more than believable in her sex scenes.

From what I've been able to put together from info on Internet chat sites and Facebook, of all places…former co-stars of Jung claim that she gave up porn and moved away. She tried to start a jewelry and antiques business with one of her male co-stars, but that soured and she apparently lives a life in relative obscurity.

THE ORAL GENERATION
1970, USA. D: Various

This is one strange oddity in crystal clear digital format (taken from what appeared to be pristine film negative). Essentially, this VS title release is a collection of (mostly) softcore short X-rated films from the dawn of the porno era. Most of the short films here all prominently feature an "Extraordinary Films" logo at the start, suggesting that these all came from the same production house. First up is "Clinical Sex", where a distraught wife complains to her doctor about the lack of sexual attention she's receiving from her husband; said doctor and his nurse take care of matters. Within the same short, another woman with sex problems gets it on with the same nurse with inflated boobs. "Any Way You Like It" finds another doc trying to help more sex-hungry women…and the shorts continue in this manner before the "The Different Sex" ends them with a few threesomes and lesbian encounters. Judging from the titles, I assume that these short films may have been disguised as "educational" sex films, when they were actually really *really* low-budget softcore titles (with the occasional look-quick-or-you'll-miss-it hardcore scene).

Then after what seems like an eternity (a fun one, mind you, because these prints are so clear and colorful you'll enjoy the stupidity despite yourself) the main feature begins. "The Oral Generation" is a fake documentary (lots of prime footage of classic 42nd street theater marquees, late-'Sixties fashion) claiming to be a scandalous reveal of the current sexual revolution of 1970. Barely over sixty minutes and your eyes will become glazed over with lots of blonde bush, firm breasts, pointy nipples, hairy swinging dicks and a narrator (in a dead serious monotone) discussing why girls are all taking to sucking dick as the 'Seventies are being ushered in. Yeah, it's that kind of movie. Bless the video archivists at VS for bringing us this one.

EXPECTATIONS
1977, USA. D: Anthony Spinelli
S: *Delania Raffino, Jack Wright, Chris Cassidy, Joey Silvera, Desiree West*

Anthony Spinelli was one of the better directors of films in this genre. Capable of making movies that combined hardcore sex and psychodramas, his were usually some of the more interesting titles. **CRY FOR CINDY** (1976), **TALK DIRTY TO ME** (1980), **NOTHING TO HIDE** (1981), and this film are among the best titles in all of porn with his 1976 feature **PORTRAIT OF SEDUCTION** (with an incredible leading performance by Vicky Lyon) as close to smut masterpiece as can be possible.

Margo (Raffino) fantasizes about encounters with men, but in reality just wants her sex life to be fulfilling. She swaps apartments and (although it's not quite clear how) lives with another woman. Margo's really unsure of what she wants out of a life, but intense sexual relations with mysterious people appear to be list highlights. Meanwhile Montana (what a name!), played by Chris Cassidy (using the pseudonym Suzette Holland!) is living in Margo's dark apartment. When Margo's eye patch-wearing brother Jack (Jack Wright) appears looking for her...it doesn't take Montana long to seduce him, and she and Jack spend the majority of the film fucking.

Meanwhile Margo goes jogging, and basically inhabits Montana's apartment with a queen-sized waterbed. Cue Joey Silvera, who appears out of nowhere (he was Montana's boyfriend) and comes by for some sex and instead finds a slightly frigid Margo. Has he noticed that Montana is no longer there and Margo instead is in her place? If he does, he doesn't let on...and suddenly the film uneasily enters Brian DePalma territory with themes of fragile minds, exchanged lives and personalities. Does this mean that Margo and her brother have an incestuous relationship as well?

After her torrid lovemaking session with Joey, Margo finds another visitor in Desiree West, resulting in a first tender, and then more slightly rough Sapphic love session. Meanwhile, Montana and Jack are still fucking.

Margo finally wants to come back to her own life and end the exchange with Montana...but Jack is happy with things as they are...and Margo becomes stuck in her new reality.

An odd film, but one with a theme that for some reason occasionally resurfaced in X-rated films of this period. Raffina was in her mid-thirties when she appeared in this film (also in two other titles, uncredited that same year), and changed her name to "Barbara Bills" in '78. In two years she appeared in six more titles then disappeared from the industry. She can also be seen in Bob Chinn's **HOT LEGS** (1979) and **CALIFORNIA GIGOLO** (1979), **CANDY GOES TO HOLLYWOOD** (1979), and Alex De Renzy's **SUMMER HEAT** (1979).

CONFESSIONS
1977, USA. D: Anthony Spinelli
S: Kristine Heller, John Leslie, Dory Devon, Joey Silvera, Sonny Landham, Desiree West

After the quasi-psychological sexual hijinks that peppered **EXPECTATIONS**, you would expect the little-known **CONFESSIONS** to be more of the same, but it's of a different ilk altogether.

Kristine Heller stars as Beth, whom we see at the opening of the movie having sensual sex with her husband, Gary (John Leslie) but after exhausting him... he turns over and to sleep. She's not done yet, and feeling frustrated, thinks back on her sexual relationship with him and deciding that he doesn't fulfill her demands in bed...she seeks pleasure elsewhere.

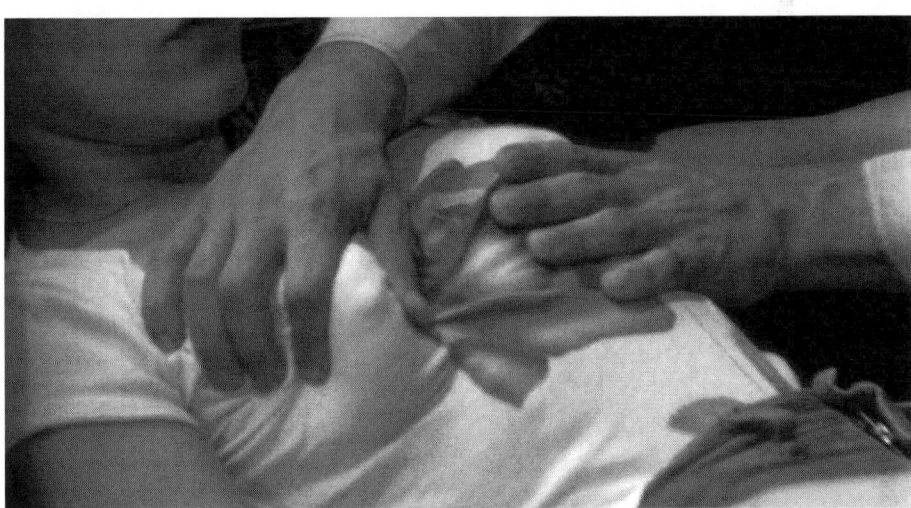

In **EXPECTATIONS** Margo (Raffino) fantasizes about encounters with men, but in reality just wants her sex life to be fulfilling...naw

Drive-In Collection

celebrate an occasion of some sort. They are throwing a party, and Joey Silvera (in suit and tie!) who plays Leslie's boss ends up in the bathroom for a devilish blowjob with Heller, and then a quick fuck as Leslie stands outside nervously guarding the door, maybe unaware of what's going on inside…maybe not.

But things go downhill from there as the storyline becomes more edgy, and the sexual couplings more imaginative. Heller spots a motorcycling leather guy (as if out of some gay S/M loop) and after few words are spoken…they are in a grim, sparsely furnished room somewhere going at it. Hired to be a dominatrix by a woman with a sub husband (Jack Wright again) things culminate when she's back home and having experienced all the passion she thinks she's been missing…is she ready to return to her bed and her husband?

The possibility of this story going full-tilt on the weirdness meter isn't immediately met here. As it's all played rather light…with some comedic touches, before taking darker turns.

John Leslie, always one of the better-trained actors in the genre really is the standout here with his supporting performance as the husband who uncomfortably seems aware of what his wife is doing. The movie's steamiest scene takes place in the couple's apartment as they

U.S. newspaper ad, from *The Village Voice* (Jan '78)

Fast 'n' Loose:
The Peculiar Pornography of Mario Siciliano

by George Pacheco

The age of the Internet has benefitted cult film fans greatly since the technology first saw its cultural rise during the 'Nineties. The power to share information across the globe with millions of people at a moment's notice is immense, and has made formerly obscure artists and performers household names amongst the legions of horror, cult and exploitation film fans the world over.

This fact...doesn't really apply to Italian director Mario Siciliano.

Indeed, there isn't much information available on the world wide web for this Roman-born director, a journeyman who—like many other individuals during the bold salad days of Italy's genre film dominance throughout the 1970s and '80s—worked throughout nearly every popular (and marketable) film style during his twenty-year career in the movie biz. Granted, Google requests and IMDb research will come up with a modicum information on the man's films, yet very little info is available on the background and filmmaking philosophies for this Italian cinema bad boy.

Siciliano worked as a writer, producer and second unit director and more during his time on the exploitation scene, serving in every conceivable capacity for the silver screen. Spaghetti Westerns, war Dramas, spy pictures, horror and *Gialli* all fell under the watchful eye of Sicilano, as the director found his creative feet as a craftsman who could deliver quick and cheap, yet with all of the salacious, exploitative trappings which were requisite for most Italian genre productions.

Mario Sicilano could perhaps, then, be compared to fellow Roman Joe D'amato, in the sense that this atmosphere of sex 'n' sleaze pervades much of his creative output from the mid-'Seventies and on through the twilight years of his career in the early 'Eighties. Siciliano helmed an astonishing *sixteen* films from 1975 to 1984—that's almost two a year—starting with his iconic horror-themed *Giallo* **EVIL EYE** (*Malocchio*, 1975) and finishing up with his insanely dirty action epic **ROLF** (a.k.a. **THE LAST MERCENARY**) in 1984.

A good chunk of these productions were hardcore pornography, often shot under the name "Lee Castle", while most of Siciliano's other genre work—such as the enjoyably sleazy 1977 Eurocrime title **THE PERFECT KILLER** (*Quel pomeriggio maledetto*, a.k.a. **THE SATANIC MECHANIC** in its cut VHS release) with Lee Van Cleef—were signed under the name of "Marlon Silko." This triple-X fare become Siciliano's bread and butter from 1980 to 1984, with

Mexican poster for **EVIL EYE** (Italy/Spain/Mexico, 1975)

the realm of pornography serving as the only film medium in which Mario would work. Until the release of **ROLF** later that year...after which the director disappeared from the public consciousness.

57

Porno character actor Giuseppe Curia

SLEAZE STYLE

Weirder still, a peculiar amount of Siciliano's adult fare would eventually find its way to Stateside VHS under the Private Screenings label, a division of Media Home Entertainment which specialized in releasing older softcore titles or triple-X edits with glamour shot model cover art and clever re-titles to fool the burgeoning video market. This meant that not only was Siciliano shooting different versions of his adult films for the international market, but that he actually managed to negotiate a distribution deal here in the States for his fast 'n' loose sex productions…Italian style.

The adult fare of Mario Siciliano was not particularly known for its production values, inventive cinematography or sense of cinematic style. No, although one could make the case for a cinematographer such as Joe D'amato utilizing some interesting shot set-ups or angles for his particular brand of pornography, Siciliano's style was substantially cheaper, sleazier and without much esoteric artistry. Instead, the director often utilized rural Italian locations—usually a villa set or otherwise secluded living area set—to tell the sort of stories one expects from low-budget porn: quick, simple and to the point.

Of course, this isn't to say that Siciliano's films didn't *have* plots; they most certainly did…just not ones which were particularly extravagant. Most of these '70s and '80s efforts were contained to one or two plot devices at a time, although some (**ORGASMO ESOTICO** [1982]) would do their best to bring into the triple-X action a bit of horror, action or mystery. Siciliano also tended to utilize a revolving cast of regulars within his casts, pruning most of the few Italian porn actors making the rounds at this early stage of the game.

CHARACTER ACTION

The most common face (and other assets) found within the adult films of Mario Siciliano had to be that of early Italian porn queen Marina Frajese, a.k.a. Marina Hedman, or Marina Lotar. This frizzy haired, voluptuous blonde bombshell was one of the few Siciliano porn actors to have a career outside of hardcore features, appearing in such films as **DELITTO A PORTA ROMANA** (a.k.a. **CRIME AT PORTA ROMANA**, 1980)—alongside legendary Italian character actor Tomas Milian—**EMANUELLE IN AMERICA** (1977), **ESCAPE FROM GALAXY 3** (*Giochi erotici nella terza galassia*, 1981), and **SCANDAL IN BLACK** (*Appuntamento in nero*, 1990).

That being said, even when Hedman did appear in non-adult features, her roles were usually limited either to brief walk-on parts or scenes which involved either nudity or hardcore inserts. Still, Hedman's feminine wiles ensured her an almost constant flow of "sexy aunt" or "sexy mother" roles, usually with some sort of predilection for seducing one of her on-screen relatives.

Believe it or not, such plot devices were fairly common in Italian films across the board, with some of Hedman's films—such as 1980's **WITH AUNT IT'S NOT A SIN** (*Con la zia non è peccato*)—selling their scandalous sleaze right in the title!

Another one of Siciliano's "motherly" types was actress Guia Lauri Filzi, a short brunette whose sexual appetite on screen was voraciously energetic when it came to bursting from the reserved roles in which she was usually cast. Filzi's dour, scowling facial features usually made these performances easy to deliver, while her up-for-anything attitude made her a favorite of many other Italian porn directors, who would usually cast her alongside such male counterparts as Mark Shannon or our next Siciliano regular…

Giuseppe Curia. Mario Siciliano's porno character actor. This mustachioed cocksmith would appear as a different stereotype in nearly every one of the director's adult features—from randy handyman to cheating fiancé—with a look which was simultaneously memorable and nondescript. Curia often served as a sexual foil for any of Siciliano's stable of willing ladies, another of which was the lithe and libidinous Laura Levi.

If Marina Hedman served as the "Edwige Fenech" of Mario Siciliano porn—busty, wanton and larger than life—then Laura Levi was the director's "Nadia Cassini" counterpart: all dark hair, come-hither eyes and shapely, erotic beauty. Levi would perform often with Siciliano stable member Karin Well in all manner of sexual shenanigans, yet the actress was also adept

DANGEROUS LOVE

at performing physical comedy as a dimwitted foil, switching from lays to laughs with ease.

Sonia Bennett is the final name I'm going to mention…even if, admittedly, not much is known about the performer, an African (American?) whose role in the Italian film industry lies solely in the world of pornography. Bennett's vibe as an actress isn't entirely dissimilar to that of Joe D'amato regular Lucia Ramirez, even if Bennett's line delivery possesses a bit more life than her severely medicated counterpart. Still, Bennett sleepwalks her way through most of these films, in nearly every respect.

THE FILMS (PART ONE)

DANGEROUS LOVE
(*Porno lui erotica lei*, 1981)

DANGEROUS LOVE may or may not be a triple-X feature. Although the version I saw would probably pass as a "hard R" softcore flick, the jagged editing and awkward cuts in the narrative lead one to believe that this 1981 film—like its contemporaries **THE OTHER WOMAN** (1981) and **HAPPY SEX** (1981)—has a harder edit out there somewhere, waiting to be discovered.

Marina Hedman is surprisingly absent here in this feature, although Karin Well does play a lead character by the name of "Marina", an heiress who serves as a sugar momma to jerky gigolo Roberto (Paolo Gramignano), who is sleeping about town with just about anything that moves. Roberto is also shacking up with *another* wealthy lady (Guia Lauri Filzi) who happens to be handicapped, in order to make the most of her fortune.

Roberto is the cad sort, and doesn't really make for a proper protagonist, while Well seems a bit detached and distracted in her performances. The sex scenes also suffer from a schizophrenic mixture of zany, sped-up comedy and slower, more romantic scenes, making for a viewing experience which begs for the fast-forward button. It's an uneven mish-mash which served as an awkward false start for Siciliano's path towards becoming a sultan of sleaze.

THE OTHER WOMAN
(*La zia svedese*, a.k.a. **MY SWEDISH AUNT**, a.k.a. **A SWEDISH SEDUCTRESS**, 1981)

THE OTHER WOMAN is probably the most well-known of Mario Siciliano's adult films, thanks to its softcore edit landing in the sweaty hands of video hounds back in the '80s from to the Private Screenings label. The film itself also possesses the most cohesive and tightly wound narrative of the bunch, and actually feels like there's a story going on, not just an interconnected series of sex scenes with a very loose plot.

This 1981 feature stars Giovanni Tamberi (under the pseudonym "Peter Thompson"[1]) as Marco, a sheltered young man who leaves his overbearing mother (Guia Lauri Filzi, in a predictable role which allows her to let down her bun hair do for a series of wanton sex scenes) for his sexually free and desirable Aunt Barbara (played, also predictably, by Marina

---

[1] IMDb erroneously credits British actor Peter Thompson (**TWINS OF EVIL** [1971]), as the star of **THE OTHER WOMAN**, presumably just a confusion caused by Tamberi's pseudonym. *–ed.*

The whole thing wraps up conveniently at the end, in typical Italian comedy fashion, with **THE OTHER WOMAN** standing as the best—and easiest to find—Siciliano sex romp. The Private Screenings VHS actually includes scenes which aren't in the adult version, while the hardcore cut naturally utilizes its running time for more scenes of shtupping between the characters...including one bizarrely edited (read: fake) dream sequence between Marina Hedman and a horse!

Don't ask.

HAPPY SEX
(*Sesso allegro*, 1981)

HAPPY SEX is another enjoyable slice of sleaze from Mario Siciliano, dealing with a trio of escaped convicts who hide out in a warehouse which just so happens to be located next door to a household of horny Italian housewives! Giuseppe Curia, Brunello Chiodetti and Paolo Gramignano are the Siciliano regulars cast as the crooks here in this "Lee Castle"-directed venture, while the eye candy is provided by Hedman, Levi and Filzi again, alongside another fixture in Italian porno (as well as their disco scene!), Sandy Samuel.

Italian poster for **HAPPY SEX**

Hedman). Tamberi's participation here is particularly notable, as the actor appeared in a number of appearances in such "legitimate" cinema as Ruggero Deodato's **PHANTOM OF DEATH** (*Un delitto poco commune*, 1988), Sergio Martino's **CASABLANCA EXPRESS** (*O Expresso de Casablanca*, 1989), and the late period Italian horror outing **SPECTERS** (*Spettri*, 1987), making this one of the rare occurrences when a Mario Siciliano player had such a comparatively esteemed career.

What's even more bizarre is that Tamberi—already physically active in the softcore cut—actually receives unsimulated oral sex from Hedman in the triple-X version! Hedman is her usual seductive self as she tries desperately to resist the sexual temptation of her nephew (by marriage), while Filzi's mother character embarks upon a journey of her own to track down Marco and bring him home...along the way succumbing to erotic urges she thought long since died with co-star Erminio Bianchi. Elsewhere, co-star Laura Levi shows her comedic skills as the bumbling maid Alice, and, for what it's worth, Levi has never looked better.

The ladies provide sex, food and companionship for the convicts, all the while planning some sort of revenge upon Ermino Bianchi again, here playing Hedman's dominant husband. To be honest, the plot is quite difficult to follow here, both from the English dub and Italian audio tracks, with much of **HAPPY SEX** jumping from one sex scene to another with lots of quick cuts and heavy handed editing. Our crooks somehow manage to ingratiate themselves into the lives of these sex-starved women and slowly begin to take control of their situation, while simultaneously avoid capture by police.

It's all done with plenty of room for slapstick comedy, sped-up camera motions and humorous sex scenes, with **HAPPY SEX** being yet another Siciliano flick which received a U.S. release on Private Screenings. This is the rare occasion, however, when the hardcore version actually does a better job at getting the film's point across than the soft edit, which is forced to cut so much sex and nudity that the plot as a whole suffers to the point of near incoherence.

The Private Screenings VHS of **HAPPY SEX** can prove difficult to track down, although a number of grey market dealers such as European Trash Cinema and Trash Palace have both soft the hardcore edits available for sale. My recommendation? Pick the XXX cut: it's less jarring and easier to enjoy.

MARINA THE NYMPHOMANIAC
(*Atteni a quelle due...ninfomani*, 1981)

This one is probably the most straightforward "pornographic" of the Mario Siciliano/"Lee Castle" features I've viewed while writing this article. All of the usual players make appearances here—Curia, Filzi, Hedman and Bianchi—alongside Sonia Bennett and Sandy Samuel again in a tale where all these people in an Italian villa talk a bunch and screw a lot.

That's about it, folks. There may be a plot here, but I'll be damned if I could understand it. It didn't help that the only copy I was able to track down from an Italian language cut with no subtitles, which made comprehending *any* of the characters motives or behavior (other than inherent silliness) nigh on impossible.

The verdict, then? Eh, perhaps worth it for a curiosity, but ultimately forgettable.

ORGASMO ESOTICO
("*Exotic Orgasm*", 1982)

ORGASMO ESOTICO is probably the most unique and original of Mario Siciliano's adult work—or, at least from the ones I've reviewed thus far—as it attempts to bridge the gap between horror and pornography, albeit with a microscopic budget.

Sonia Bennett plays some sort of mystical temptress who, alongside her lover/slave/cohort Marina Hedman are seducing strangers, murdering them and throwing them down a well in their backyard. These victims then rise from the well as the horny living dead, looking for revenge with a bit of hardcore sex on the side! Trust me, you haven't lived until you've seen a made-up Marina Hedman giving head as the dead!

Sure, the affair *does* get a bit predictable at times, but the cheap, sleazy atmosphere is there, while the badass soundtrack steals wholesale from other Italian productions, including Marcello Giombini's score for the Joe D'amato flick **ABSURD** (*Rosso sangue*, 1981)! There's torture, there's sex, there's awkward acting and even more awkward storytelling, making **ORGASMO ESOTICO** *the* Siciliano flick to choose for those who are seeking a little horror with their porn.

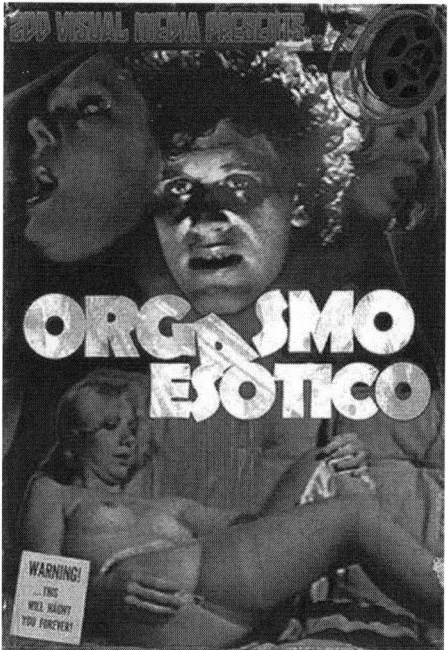

Top: Italian poster. **Above:** Anglo video cover

AUTHOR'S NOTE: These Mario Siciliano films are extremely difficult to find, particularly in their uncut Italian versions. Bootleg/Grey Market DVDs are the only way to go here (or the softcore versions released on VHS via Private Screenings) with no sight of any proper home video releases on the horizon any time soon. Hell, I'm *still* trying to find the other five films in this series for Part Two of my article, so if you're looking to catch any of the titles we discussed here, hit up your local, reputable Grey Market man for the goods!

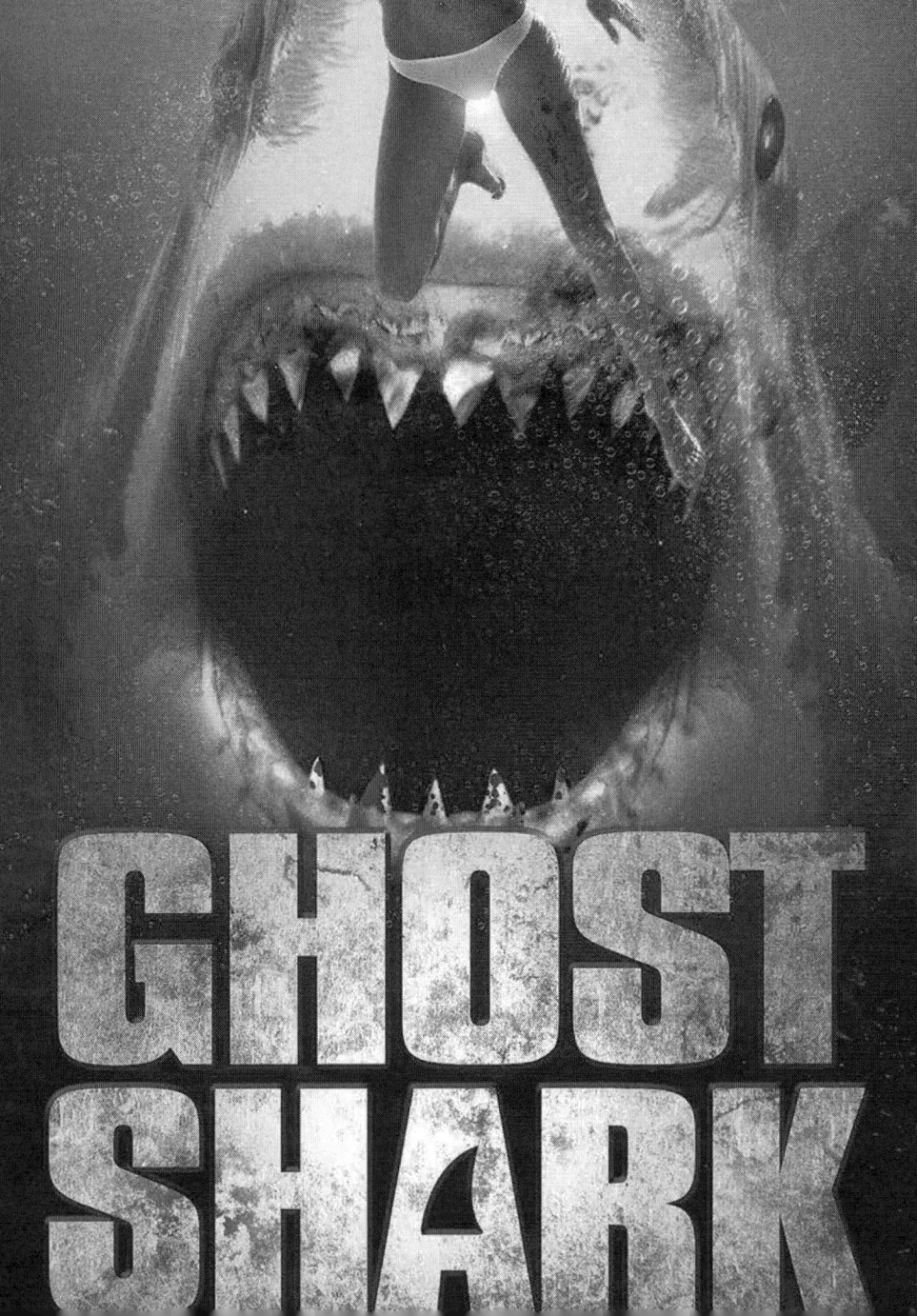

JUMPING THEMSELVES:
6 HEAD-SLAPPING SHARK TAILS!

by Brian Harris

"Show me the way to go home
I'm tired and I want to go to bed
I had a little drink about an hour ago
And it's gone right to my head
Wherever I may roam
By land or sea or foam
You can always hear me singing this song

Show me the way to go home.
Show me the way to go home
I'm tired and I want to go to bed

I had a little drink about an hour ago
And it's gone right to my head
Wherever I may roam
On land or sea or foam
You can always hear me singing this..."

"...start the engines."

No other cinematic experience, outside of **THE EXORCIST** and the Star Wars trilogy, has so thoroughly captured the imagination and stoked the fear of a generation than Steven Spielberg's 1975 masterpiece of mayhem **JAWS**. It quite literally scarred Americans, sending them running from beaches and the water, and instigated an irrational fear of the Great White Shark globally that can be felt even to this day. It's a powerful piece of cinema featuring tried-and-true "man versus nature" and "animals gone amok" formulas still being used by filmmakers. When it comes to killer sea-life films, **JAWS** simply cannot be topped; many filmmakers have attempted to, but no matter how hard they try, they simply cannot recreate the sheer, unadulterated terror Spielberg brought to the big screen. As one might expect, that certainly hasn't stopped them from trying over and over, though. Even the Italians tried to get in on some of that action at one time!

There have been dozens of **JAWS** rip-offs down through the years, some have been good (**DEEP BLUE SEA** [1999], **OPEN WATER** [2003]), others not so good (**JAWS: THE REVENGE** [1987], **SHARK ZONE** [2003]). Hell, not all have even used sharks; some have featured piranha (**PIRANHA** [1978], **PIRANHACONDA** [2012]), barracuda (**BARRACUDA** [1978]), alligators (**ALLIGATOR** [1980], **LAKE PLACID** [1999]), whales (**ORCA** [1977]) and octopuses/squid (**TENTACLES** [1977], **THE BEAST** [1996]). Whatever works (or doesn't), right?

While the crazier shark films have been around for quite awhile, it wasn't until Roger Corman's slab of mix 'n' match shark insanity **SHARKTOPUS** (2010) and Anthony C. Ferrante's 2013 "shark out of water" mind-blower **SHARKNADO** did people really realize that the shark film had pulled an Arthur Fonzarelli. Want to hear the best part? People went crazy for them! Not only has **SHARKNADO** received a sequel, **SHARKNADO 2: THE SECOND ONE** (2014), but Syfy and The Asylum are working on a

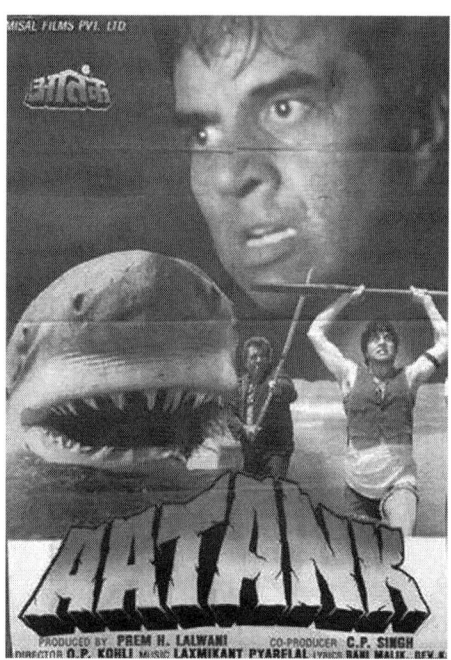

There was even an Indian **JAWS** rip-off from 1996 called **AATANK**

the world of this mouthy menace falls on the shoulders of the United States Navy and Admiral Engleberg (Matt Lagan). Their only hope lies with deep sea sub specialists Jack Turner (Christopher Judge), his wife Rosie (Elisabeth Röhm) and their computer navigation program NERO (Voiced by Paul Anderson). If NERO can be installed inside a massive mechanical shark constructed by the Navy, with Rosie piloting and Jack handling remote navigation, they just might have a chance of defeating the Mega. That is, if something doesn't go wrong and they lose control of the Mecha Shark. Oh yeah…they *totally* lose control of the Mecha Shark! It's Mega versus Mecha for the fate of the world!

It's hard to believe the *Mega Shark Vs.* series is already on number three, but here it is and without a doubt it has come the furthest. The production design was impressive, as was the CG, and the acting is surprisingly good, especially from leads Judge (*Stargate SG-1*) and Röhm (**LAKE PLACID: THE FINAL CHAPTER** [2012]). There were a few sequences that had a *Power Rangers* VFX feel to me, but for the most part **MEGA SHARK VS. MECHA SHARK** is a hard B-movie to hate. But—there's always one of those, right?—it is missing something, though, the single most important ingredient required to make or break a B-movie, and that would be *FUN*. **MEGA SHARK VS. MECHA SHARK** isn't all that fun, and it really should be! You've got a giant shark and a giant mechanical shark equipped with a *Night Rider* "KITT" personality (NERO); I'm not saying there's endless possibilities there, but if you're going to take notes from Mechagodzilla and Mechani-Kong, you've got to include the fun! I suppose I could also make mention of the long, tension-free battles but honestly I think those were only noticeable because of the low entertainment value.

Not a bad film by any means—it felt bigger than its budget—but it just doesn't have that *"Wow! Cool!"* factor a film like this should. A real missed opportunity to go balls-out nutty that instead comes off like a skipping record. Bueller…Bueller…Bueller…

third film! And what of Roger Corman's **SHARKTOPUS**? Same deal, **SHARKTOPUS VS. PTERACUDA** (2014) has already seen release and Corman & Co. are hard at work on **SHARKTOPUS VS. MERMANTULA** (2015). Before you scoff, consider this, **SHARKNADO 2: THE SECOND ONE** pulled in over 3.9 million viewers! Even if it wasn't you tuning in, somebody is watching! (It's me!)

For the purposes of this article, I decided to select six shark films from the *"What did I just watch?"* category that aren't **SHARKNADO** or **SHARKTOPUS**. Their qualities range from "stupid as hell" to "you gotta be kidding", and they're all just waiting to be enjoyed by the not-so-picky B-movie fan. I even included one that can only be described as "how is this not in theaters?!". Don't over-think them, don't try to poke holes through their logic because none of them really contain any…just kick back and enjoy!

MEGA SHARK VS. MECHA SHARK (2014)

When a massive glacier weakens while being transported by tug through the warm waters of Port of Alexandria, Egypt, the contents trapped inside are unleashed, spilling forth a ferocious, Cenozoic creature, the Megalodon! Hungry and horny, the Mega goes on a terror spree through the oceans of the world, bringing all commercial fishing and water-bound imports/exports to a grinding halt. With the global economy on the verge of collapse, the responsibility of ridding

HAMMERHEAD: SHARK FRENZY (2005)
(a.k.a. **SHARKMAN**, a.k.a. **HAMMERHEAD**)

A corporate CEO and a hand-picked group of employees, including a biologist and the head of the IT department, head to a remote island by invitation of scientist Dr. Preston King (Jeffrey Combs). While the group believes they're there to witness King's breakthrough in the cure for cancer, King himself has other plans, namely making them all pay for their roles in his ousting from the corporation and disgrace from the scientific community. The true nature of his work is far more sinister than seeking a cure for cancer; King has created a man/hammerhead shark hybrid that he intends to mate with a human woman, in essence creating a new species of man. But first, he wants revenge! Instead of partying and enjoying the tropical paradise, the group finds themselves trapped on an island with no escape or way to call for help, and a bloodthirsty sharkman stalking them!

HAMMERHEAD is actually a fun flick; I mean you've got a mad scientist, gross shark fetuses, shark rape (you don't get to see it, pervs!) and quite a few nasty, gory surprises. It was nice to see Combs reprising his role as Herbert West (not really, but close), and though William Forsythe isn't what I'd call leading man material (especially with that beer gut hanging out), it's always nice to see him as well. Thankfully, the film doesn't spend too much time on characterization; shit hits the fan pretty quick and before you know it you're in the thick of the genetically modified jungle and the sharkman is on the warpath. The one thing I did find myself wondering while watching this was, where did all these damn characters learn their guerrilla warfare skills? Was it taught at some corporate retreat between potato salad sampling and trust exercises? Seriously! A bunch of paper-pushers and a tech geek are able to shoot, hit targets, fly choppers, make booby traps and all sorts of shit. It was like a MacGuyver convention!

Nu Image does low budget action, horror and sci-fi and whether you like their shit or not, they feel real. The CG is decent, real vehicles are used like actual helicopters, they even feature real explosions. They feel real, therefore they're a bit more entertaining for me. They remind me of the Filipino action films of the '80s. They could have done with a bit more full-on shots of the sharkman but it is what it is and if you can find this for $5 and under, it's a steal!

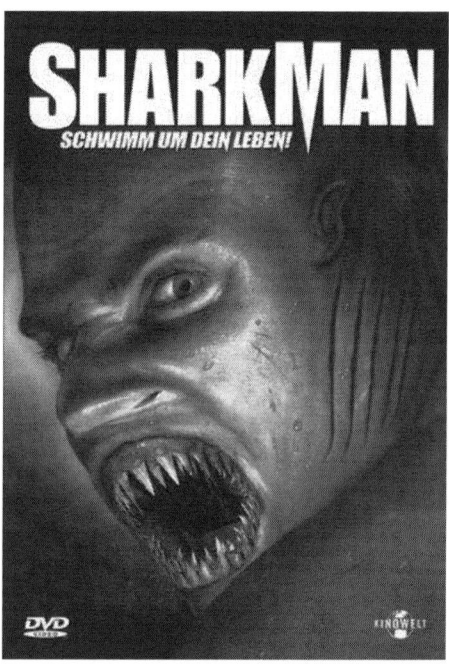

German DVD for
HAMMERHEAD: SHARK FRENZY

By the way, before hitting the net for answers, an AK-47 can indeed shoot underwater.

2-HEADED SHARK ATTACK (2012)

A boatload of college kids hoping to score some credits in a nautical education class get more than they bargained for when the carcass of a megamouth shark gets caught in their propeller and damages the hull.

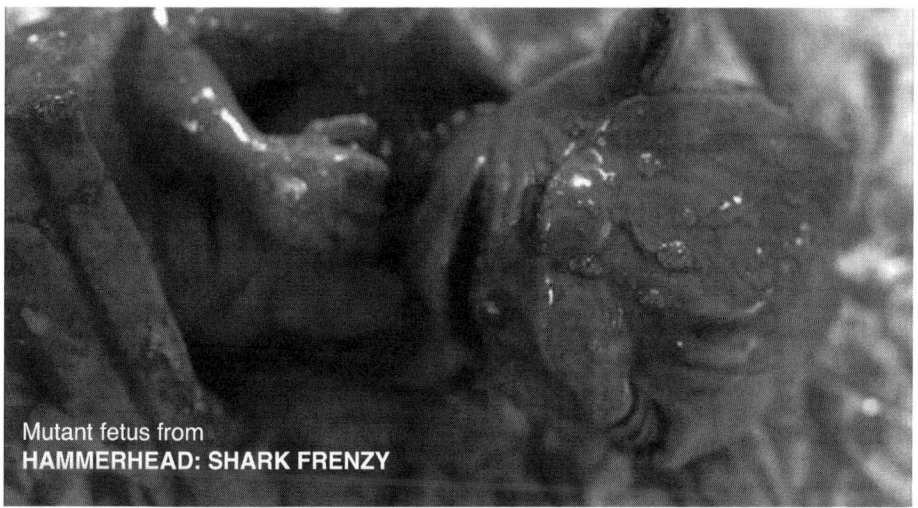

Mutant fetus from
HAMMERHEAD: SHARK FRENZY

Sure there's is a shark monster in **2-HEADED SHARK ATTACK**, but there are also boobs

Forced to go ashore a tiny abandoned atoll while repairs are being made, the situation only worsens when quakes begin hitting the island, indicating that the atoll's coral foundation is collapsing. As if that weren't enough, the waters are no longer safe either as they find themselves being picked off by a ferocious great white shark...*WITH TWO HEADS!* Double the mutation, double the danger and teeth! The race is on to figure out a way off the dying island and out of the water, but wherever they go the 2-headed shark is sure to follow!

What can you say about a film called **2-HEADED SHARK ATTACK**? Does it give you a shark? Yes. Did it have two heads? Sure did. Did it attack people with its two heads? Yeah, actually it did! The film provides us with an actual two-headed shark (both CG and practical FX), a boatload of big breasts, a douchebag, the awkward nerd, a sassy black girl, a few slags, and Brooke Hogan accompanied by a chin that puts the state of Florida to shame. I mean, you really get everything you'd expect in this film so it's pretty hard to hate on it. The only thing I can say is that Hogan's "backstory" and her constant willingness to jump into the water and fix everything with an engine were at odds and came off convoluted and silly.

Carmen Electra was looking a little worse for the wear and O'Connell is a pimp; outside of that you should expect nothing but a roaring—*yes, roaring*—shark with two heads and Hogan pretty much playing MacGuyver, Quint, The A-Team and Sheriff Brody all in one barely clothed character.

My suggestion for a sequel is to skip 3-HEADED SHARK ATTACK altogether and go to 4-HEADED SHARK FRENZY and call it a day.

SAND SHARKS (2011)

Small-time conman and deadbeat Jimmy Green (Corin Nemec) is back in town with another harebrained get-rich-quick scheme for his father, Mayor Greenburg (Edgar Allan Poe IV), to consider. In order to drum up business for the locals on the island, Jimmy lays out his plan to throw a huge spring break party that would provide live music and accommodate spring breakers with camp grounds, toilets, the works. Against his better judgment, Mayor Greenburg agrees and places Jimmy in charge of the entire operation, including securing financiers, promoting, hiring lighting technicians and finding musicians.

It's going to be a blast like no other, but there appears to be one little hitch...there may or may not have been another shark attack. The problem with this particular attack is that body parts are found in the sand, away from the water and high tide, and an eyewitness even claims to have seen her boyfriend attacked by a shark...a shark that came from the sand! Impossible, you say? The sheriff and his deputies aren't convinced either but as the party's launch nears, the "sand sharks" reveal themselves in a big, bloody way. Can the Mayor, sheriff and Jimmy, with the help of Brooke Hogan's tree trunk legs, stop the sand sharks before they devour the entire town?

Wait, so, the sharks are sand sharks or are they sharks in the sand? The answer is...*yes. Oh, look, a shiny penny!* But seriously, this film is about sharks swimming around in the sand. It's fucking stupid by all measures and yet it still succeeded in putting a smile on my face. Sure, some of the

CG was shit, including some of the kills, and the acting was bad, and the "giant party" really only consisted of maybe fifty extras spread out a few feet away from one another. Wait…what was I saying…oh, so yeah, sure this is a bad film; Nemec shits it up with so much hardcore ham it's hard to take this stupid concept even remotely serious, but then why in hell would you anyhow? I mean, it's about sharks that swim in sand! Brooke Hogan makes an appearance as a oceanologist or sharkiatrist, who knows, but she's in here and it's hard to decide whether she's attractive or looks too much like a vaginal version of The Hulkster. Either way, she's an awful actress. Thankfully there's a Crazy Ralph/Quint-type doing his best impression of Burgess Meredith to keep our eyes from straying to Hogan's butt-chin. Nemec and the sharks are the draw here, no doubt about it, and if that's what you come for, you're going to love this film. Except you…probably won't.

Let this one-liner spoken by Hogan sink in for just a moment: "Eat this you sand of a bitch!"

GHOST SHARK (2013)

A shark fatally wounded by an angry fisherman's grenade makes its way into a cave filled with symbols on the walls, and it dies. Turns out, the cave is cursed and anything that dies by violence within it is returned to the world of the living as a vengeful ghost! A group of young people discover the existence of this spectral shark but nobody believes them, even as bodies pile up. With a re-election on the way, the Mayor is determined to have the perpetrator of these gory murders caught, but this murder monster is on a mission to extinguish all human life. Only the spells in an ancient book and the knowledge of the town's old lighthouse keeper can defeat the ghost shark but the book is missing and the lighthouse keeper is lost in a bottle!

When they say "Get out of the water!" they mean "Get out of all water!"

Outside of the next film on my list, **GHOST SHARK** is one of my favorites. The title says it all: there's a shark's ghost haunting a town and eating anybody within the slightest distance from water. It's just able to appear wherever there's water,

Actress Alice Krige attenps to bring some class to **TRICK OR...SHARK!**

which means the shark kills people in pools, standing in open hydrants, sliding on a Slip 'N Slide, getting their car washed, fixing plumbing, sitting on the toilet, *even drinking from a dixie cup!* Nobody is safe, and I mean nobody, even children die horribly! What could possibly make this film more entertaining? A mixture of both CG and practical FX! I'm almost 100% positive that close-ups of the snapping shark are a hand puppet! So fucking fun!

The "all-star" lineup for this insane film includes Richard Moll (*Night Court*) as the Crazy Ralph, Mackenzie Rosman (*7th Heaven*) as a lifeless automaton and YouTube quasi-celeb Shawn C. Phillips playing the whiny, hungry fat guy. For the most part, Moll carries the film. Thankfully, he doesn't need to carry the entire thing because we're watching this heap for one thing, and one thing only: *the vengeful ghost of a shark that has been wronged by a fisherman with grenades.* My god, that sounds stupid, but it actually works...with beer, or weed, or an insane amount of boredom that can only be cured by comical dismemberment.

I'm not at all sure why this damn film isn't out on DVD/BD in the States, but it isn't. Bad move, Asylum! *This shit is mad fun!* Oh, there's also a shit one-liner which is nowhere near as fun as the one-liner from **SAND SHARKS**. It goes a little something like this: "Bitch me, you bitch." Yeah, that's shit.

TRICK OR...SHARK! (2014)
(a.k.a. **MELVILLE'S PASSING**)

A group of "way-too-old to trick 'r treat" teens decide to play a cruel prank on an old woman (Alice Krige) rumored to be a witch in their seaside town. The prank leads to the tragic accidental death of the woman's only friend, a small dog by the name of Melville. Though the teens are apprehended and caught by the local constable (Michael Parks), the old woman is inconsolable over the loss and unwilling to accept the apologies offered by the teens. Deciding their punishment should fit their crime, she retrieves a centuries old book hidden in her cellar and calls forth an ancient demon from the watery depths, with the head of a shark and the body of a man!

Halloween will never be the same again for this small town, as the monster stalks its unsuspecting prey in the open, surrounded by costumes, candy and the squeals of children.

While director Justin A. Prellep obviously lifted his film's premise from the classic **PUMPKINHEAD** (1988), Prellep still manages to make it his own, one could almost smell the leaves burning and the sea salt in the air during some sequences. Surprisingly, **TRICK OR...SHARK!** was shot on 16mm, not digital, and all of the effects, including the outstanding shark demon, were practical FX. While I try never to judge films by their use of CG, it is really nice to see filmmakers still doing it the old fashion way. The title—yeah, it's cheesy—was changed by the distribution company, prompting Prellep to pull the film before it hit the market. Only a lucky few critics received review copies. According to the director, he'll be releasing it himself and will be going with the original title, **MELVILLE'S PASSING**.

Did I like this film? No, I loved it. It's crazy good Lovecratian filmmaking, thick with fog and atmosphere, the shots of seaside cliffs are breathtaking, the creature is freakin' sweet and Prellep doesn't skimp on gore. This is one hell of an insane shark film right here! It's like a combination of the aforementioned **PUMPKINHEAD**, plus **DEAD & BURIED** (1981), **DAGON** (2001), and **SATAN'S LITTLE HELPER** (2005).

—

So there you have it, I saved the best two films for last as they provided me with the most entertainment! Just remember, if your shark film doesn't include *a skeptical sheriff*, *a mayor unwilling to close the beaches* and *a shit-ton of human chum*, you're missing out. Hopefully, you check out these films and decide for yourself whether they're simply amazing, simply bad, or a whole lot of both! Happy Hunting, *ARRR!*

MEGA SHARK VS. MECHA SHARK
2014, USA. D: EMILE EDWIN SMITH
AVAILABLE FROM THE ASYLUM

HAMMERHEAD
2005, ARUBA/USA/GERMANY. D: MICHAEL OBLOWITZ
AVAILABLE FROM MILLENNIUM

2-HEADED SHARK ATTACK
2012, USA. DIRECTOR: CHRISTOPHER RAY
AVAILABLE FROM THE ASYLUM

SAND SHARKS
2011, USA. DIRECTOR: MARK ATKINS
AVAILABLE FROM PHASE 4 FILMS

GHOST SHARK
2013, USA. DIRECTOR: GRIFF FURST
AVAILABLE FROM SIGNATURE ENTERTAINMENT [R2/B]

TRICK OR…SHARK!
2014, USA. DIRECTOR: JUSTIN A. PRELLEP
AVAILABLE FROM PESCADENTE RELEASING

"Why Don't You Ask Him If He's Going to Stay?"
Taking **TUSK** On Its Own Terms

by Stephen R. Bissette

Kevin Smith's **TUSK** *(2014) was worth the four-hour-round-trip to catch it in its fleeting theatrical release at the closest multiplex showing this whacked gem; woe to those who missed it.*

This review is precisely what I'd avoided reading beforehand.

I went in knowing nothing about it—I don't listen to Kevin's podcasts—and kept it that way, and just went for the ride. So, my recommendation is to avoid reading this review until after you've seen **TUSK** yourself.

I can't put it any simpler than this: this is what going to the movies should be like!

SPOILER ALERT: it's impossible to discuss **TUSK** without spoiling something, honestly, but I'll do my best for this first page.

Once you turn the page, we'll be tipping some ashtrays, spilling some beans, and showing some hands, even though I'm trying my best not to. It's a certainty that in illustrating this analysis, my editors will reveal too much. If there were a way to contrive to bind the pages together, forcing you to cut them apart to read this, I would find a way to do that—but that's not viable.

Look, just take my word for it: If you love outrageous horror movies, stop reading right now, and just see **TUSK** first by whatever means necessary or possible (and there, I've already said too much).

Then again, if you love Kevin Smith movies, that means you've most likely heard the fateful *SModcast* podcast and/or participated fully in the twitter decision and crowd funding campaigns (#Walrusyes from @ThatKevinSmith) and already know what **TUSK** is and from whence it sprang.

In that case, you're already in—and in on—the movie.

TUSK is Smith's latest opus, and oh what an opus it is. Not wanting to give away the game(s) but wanting to write a proper assessment creates quite a quandary. I'll be coy, but it's an ungainly and impossible task.

Smith and his creative team and cast pool their considerable resources and pull off a savvy, relatively low-budget (by 2014 standards), punch-drunk, and frankly astonishing genre effort that works beautifully—as an exercise in absurdist surgical horror, as a cautionary satire for Podcasters everywhere, and as a ruthless parody of this past decade's cinematic genre abuses.

If you don't dig it, well, what can I say? This was my cup of tea (oops, spoiler #1)...

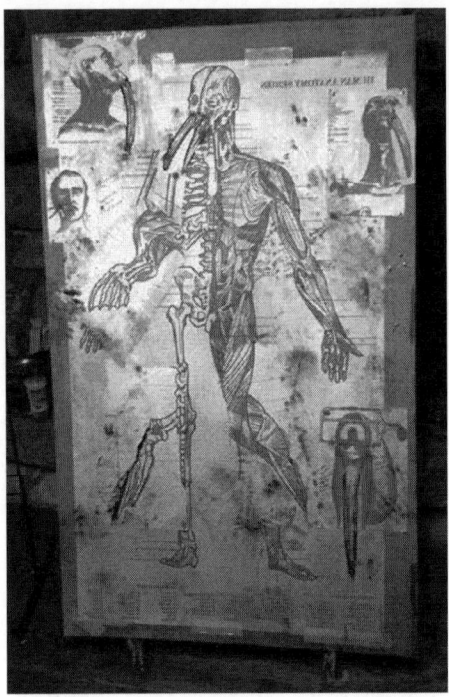

Smith cooked this up effortlessly (truly: the script was improvised on-air as a *SModcast* riff on a Gumtree prank sex ad/post—a prank, it turned out, by Brighton poet Chris Parkinson, who earned an associate producer credit here—hence the dubious "based on a true story" title announcement/warning) plundering a century of "mad doctor" rural horror pulp, comics, and movies clichés. Pirating those clichés while unflinchingly sticking to its comedic guns, **TUSK** is essentially a pinnipedal revamp of everything from Gaston Leroux's novel *Balaoo* (1911) to movies from Sam Newfield's **THE MAD MONSTER** (1942) to **SSSSSSS!** (1973), with Michael Parks in the George Zucco/Strother Martin role.

Michael Parks—who was, let us not forget, John Huston's Adam in **THE BIBLE: IN THE BEGINNING** (1966)—makes the most of the role, as had Zucco and dear old Strother, too. In one way, Parks is riffing on every one of moviedom's isolated, predatory rural mad doctors since Lon Chaney established the archetype in **THE MONSTER** (1925)—and seriously, **THE MONSTER** is *the* template for **TUSK**, absolutely. In another way, he is spinning off his memorable TV turn as the vengeful Canadian silent partner on One-Eyed Jacks in David Lynch and Mark Frost's *Twin Peaks* TV series (1990-91), and if that alone doesn't get your ass into a theater or home theater seat, nothing will.

Let's see: if we're going to play the name game, we can dance around spoilers a wee bit. Smith knows his shit: this is **FREAKS** (1932) by way of **CALVAIRE** (2004), and resonates as richly with Smith's wicked sense of play and humor pitched to the fore. **TUSK** would have been an ideal 1970s drive-in opus—and it is that, in spades, joining **CREATURE** (2011) as my favorite recent American monster movie that knows exactly what the hell it wants to be, puts all its resources up on the screen, and doesn't let up or back off.

In 1973 drive-in movie terms, Smith spins on **THE STRANGE VENGEANCE OF ROSALIE** (Jack Starrett/Anthony Greville-Bell and John Kohn's adaptation of Miles Tripp's novel *The Chicken*) by way of Bernard L. Kowalski/Hal Dresner/Daniel C. Striepeke's **SSSSSSS!**, with Robert Kurtzman and his **TUSK** team's makeup FX (supplant pinniped obsession for the reptilian obsession) playing as key a role as John Chambers (and Striepeke) did for the latter. In more Millennial movie terms, for those with shorter memories, it's **MISERY** (1990) loves company of **THE HUMAN CENTIPEDE (FIRST SEQUENCE)** (2009)…oh but don't let that put you off. Don't avoid **TUSK** fearing more of the brand of **THE PASSION**/Bush/Cheney-era "extraordinary rendition" nastiness the *Saw* series reveled in, because believe you me, Smith's got your number, too, as well as theirs.

—

Michael Parks makes **TUSK** essential viewing. For my generation (I turn 60 in 2015), Parks is forever Bus Riley (**BUS RILEY'S BACK IN TOWN**, [1965]) and above all the motorcycling hero of the TV series *Then Came Bronson* (1969-70), his TV-theme-song Top-40 hit (which also scored 41st for country that year) "Long Lonesome Highway" launching a short-lived recording career with MGM before his stint as Philip Colby on TV's *Dynasty* spawned *The Colbys* (1986-87). For most of my peers, Parks seemed to disappear other than that, but for me, he was omnipresent in the unlikeliest places: playing Robert F. Kennedy for Larry Cohen's **THE PRIVATE FILES OF J. EDGAR HOOVER** (1977), directing and starring in (the title role Clint Eastwood defined) **THE RETURN OF JOSEY WALES** (1986), as the Irish crime lord up against the real Bronson (Charles) in Michael Winner's **DEATH WISH V: THE FACE OF DEATH** (1994), and beautifully playing one of my all-time-favorite authors, Ambrose Bierce, in the sorely underrated **FROM DUSK TILL DAWN 3: THE HANGMAN'S DAUGHTER** (2000). But for most readers, Parks popped the radar playing the insidious French-Canadian criminal Jean Renault in *Twin Peaks* and Texas Ranger Earl McGraw for Robert Rodriguez and Quentin Tarantino in **FROM DUSK TILL DAWN** (1996), **KILL BILL: VOL. 1** (2003; Parks played Estaban Vihaio in **KILL BILL: VOL. 2**, 2004, all referenced in **TUSK** via the central narrative function of the Kill Bill Kid, played by Douglas Banks), and **GRINDHOUSE** (2007, both features—and note that his real-life son, James Parks, played McGraw's son in **KILL BILL, FROM DUSK TILL DAWN 2: TEXAS BLOOD MONEY**, and **GRINDHOUSE**). I'll forever rue the day his role as the late, great comics creator Jack Kirby was trimmed from **ARGO** (2012), but that's hardly Parks' fault, is it?

Parks has quietly blistered the screen in numerous genre outings since 2000, but his most recent turns for Smith as fanatical Pastor Abin Cooper for **RED STATE** (2011) and as Howard Howe in **TUSK** elevate him even further into the stellar pantheon of cinema crazies (add to this Parks' role as Doc Barrows in Jim Mickle and Nick Damici's **WE ARE WHAT WE ARE**, the 2013 remake of Jorge Michel Grau's harrowing **SOMOS LO QUE HAY** [2010]). Parks is in top form in **TUSK**. It's almost impossible, given the utterly absurd premise of **TUSK** and specifically Parks' role, to claim he is underplaying the part, but damned if he isn't. By turns sly, sinister, and hilarious as the most attentive but loopiest host imaginable, Parks coaxes both the unwary hero and the audience into the web with considerable guile, and keeps toying with his and our affections to the bitter end. Though few have seen fit to notice or (if they have) comment upon it, but we're seeing a renaissance of 1930s-1940s poverty-row mad doctors of late, amped to the max—and I'd place Parks' Howard Howe up there as the contemporary George Zucco to, say, Dieter Laser's Peter Lorre of Tom Six's **THE HUMAN CENTIPEDE (FIRST SEQUENCE)**. The latter is indeed the closest associative companion to **TUSK** in many ways, including the twisted "master and his pet" obsessions/relationships central to both films, but there's a world of difference between the how far both filmmakers dare to go, to what ends, and which edges they drive us over. Like director Kevin Smith (compared to Tom Six), Parks plays the gentleman in **TUSK**, even as he tips his hand about his fixations, his madness, and his true colors, and that's the performance that really makes Smith's insane little potboiler simmer and roil.

Keeping pace with Michael Parks doing the ultimate 21st century George Zucco resurrection, Smith assembled a terrifically game cast, with Justin Long, Haley Joel Osment, and Genesis Rodriguez (Génesis Rodríguez Pérez) as the gender-inversion-of-**PSYCHO** (1960) leads (this time, it's a guy's fate-worse-than-death disappeared that brings out an unlikely couple and investigator in search of the truth). They each bring their own baggage to their roles, as is right and proper in every Kevin Smith movie.

Génesis Rodríguez Pérez is the loving girlfriend who has had quite enough of her beau's insensitive shit, but can't help but fret over his disappearance and propel the investigation that drives the second and third acts; for those who only know her from her feature film roles (debuting in **MAN ON A LEDGE** [2012], followed by **WHAT TO EXPECT WHEN YOU'RE EXPECTING** the same year and **THE LAST STAND, IDENTITY THIEF**, and **HOURS** in 2013), Génesis is the Traci Lords of Telemundo infamy. English-speaking

The Doctor is In: That's not needlepoint Howard Howe (Michael Parks) is threading in Kevin Smith's **TUSK**—and we're not going to show you what he's up to

Old Wine, New Bottle: **TUSK**'s Howard Howe takes his cues from Lon Chaney/ Dr. Gustave Ziska's bedside manner in Roland West, Willard Mack and Albert Kenyon's adaptation of Crane Wilbur's **THE MONSTER** (1925)

American soap opera viewers first saw Rodríguez Pérez in *The Days Of Our Lives* (2005-2006), but she had actually debuted in the Telemundo network's telenovelas *Prisionera* (2004) at age 16 and was involved in a scandalous love affair with her telenovela co-star Mauricio Islas (then aged 30 and married), resulting in an out-of-court settlement that kept Islas out of prison and earned Génesis millions (including a major windfall from Telemundo). Génesis openly riffed on that notoriety with her role in **CASA DE MI PADRE** (2012), and she brings kittenish candor to her role in **TUSK** that lends some emotional resonance to the whole giddy concoction (her character here is also not above using her sexuality to coax a confession at one point out of her boyfriend).

Haley Joel Osment's genre credentials are indelibly, almost genetically coded into anyone who grew up with **BOGUS** (1996), **THE SIXTH SENSE** (1999), **A.I.** (a.k.a. **A.I. ARTIFICIAL INTELLIGENCE**, [2001]), and direct-to-video Disney fare like **BEAUTY AND THE BEAST: THE ENCHANTED CHRISTMAS** (1997), **THE HUNCHBACK OF NOTRE DAME II**, **THE COUNTRY BEAR** (both 2002), and **THE JUNGLE BOOK 2** (2003). Osment survived his share of post-child-star tabloid scandal (his 2006 auto accident, suffering minor injuries while drunk and carrying, pleading no contest for DUI and drug possession and the usual probation/rehab/fine/AA penalties), and his current career reboot is enhanced by his role here and in Smith's forthcoming **YOGA HOSERS**, the second in a proposed trilogy set in Canada (with Osment reportedly playing Smith's fictionalized surrogate for infamous anti-Semitic fascist journalist and self-proclaimed Canadian *Führer* Adrien Arcand, putting him in league with Michael Parks previous role for Smith in **RED STATE**).

Always affable Justin Long earned his genre stripes early in his career with the one-two punch of **GALAXY QUEST** (1999) and **JEEPERS CREEPERS** (2001, with a cameo in its 2003 sequel), followed by roles in **THE SASQUATCH GANG** (2006, a.k.a. **THE SASQUATCH DUMPLING GANG**), **IDIOCRACY** (2006), **DRAG ME TO HELL** (2009) and more. Long's only tabloid turns have been tied to his relationships—with Drew Barrymore and of late with Amanda Seyfried—having completely skirted taint-by-association with **JEEPERS CREEPERS** director Victor Salva, but his squeaky-clean rep justifiably stands, and that lends his adventurous onscreen role here rich resonance: Long and Smith play off and against Long's persona.

Long suffers the brunt of **TUSK**'s torments, on and offscreen (consider, if you will, the makeup sessions he must have endured), playing podcaster Wallace Bryton as the insensitive-but-likable asshole who pays beyond the ultimate price for his narcissistic hubris.
And oh, does he pay.

It's a fearless performance and a lot of fun, especially once Long's most recognizable boyish attributes are buried. Like Christopher Lee's Kharis in Terence Fisher's **THE MUMMY** (1959), by the final acts all Long is left to work with onscreen are his eyes—the very eyes the Creeper (Jonathan Breck) lusted after in **JEEPERS CREEPERS**—and he delivers to the last shot.

—

As I noted earlier, the roles here are a gender inversion of those in Robert Bloch's and Alfred Hitchcock/Joseph Stefano's **PSYCHO** (the novel and the film). Closer to the roots, what Smith and his cronies have concocted here is an extreme spin on Roland West's venerable chestnut **THE MONSTER**, West's adaptation of Crane Wilbur's play (co-scripted with Willard Mack and Albert Kenyon). That essentially-forgotten silent vehicle for Lon Chaney cast Chaney as Gustave Ziska, a backwoods renegade surgeon whose capture of a young woman (Gertrude Olmstead)—the latest in a procession of mysterious disappearances and kidnappings—prompts her lover (Johnny Arthur), his co-worker (Hallam Cooley), and a local constable (Charles Sellon) to trace her disappearance and hopefully rescue her from Ziska's mad experiments in an "abandoned" asylum.

Like **TUSK**, **THE MONSTER** was first and foremost a comedy, too. You see, the setup and template was just that familiar in the 1920s, already!

Crane Wilbur's play's pulp scenario has fueled countless horror films and horror film parodies since, from James Whale's **THE OLD DARK HOUSE** (1932) to Georges Franju/Jean Redon/Pierre Boileau/Thomas Narcejac/Claude Sautet's **LES YEUX SANS VISAGE** (a.k.à. **EYES WITHOUT A FACE**, a.k.a. **THE HORROR CHAMBER OF DR. FAUSTUS**, 1960/1962) and all the spin-offs of and riffs on those classics. It's telling both of the nature of genre, and of Kevin Smith's affection for and knowledge of the genre, that Smith could just spit out this comedic claptrap so gleefully with Scott Mosier in one sitting of his *SModcast* (give it a listen: *http://smodcast.com/episodes/the-walrus-and-the-carpenter/*). Yes, we *all* know this story—but you've never heard or experienced this version, even after you've tuned into the *SModcast*. There's many a mile twixt the lip and the cup (or, in this case, **TUSK**), and the fun is in the telling.

The most volatile career baggage of anyone onscreen is something I can't go into without the ultimate spoiler alert. Suffice to note **TUSK**'s key role of Guy LaPointe, the ex-police investigator, boasts the funniest casting coup since Ortiz the Dog Boy in Alex Winter and Tom Stern's **FREAKED** (1993, oddly enough the movie I most wanted to revisit after **TUSK**). The cat's been out of the bag since the movie opened, but I won't give that game away, either, save to say it added enormously to the perverse fun.

For all the cozy familiarity duly noted with the narrative template, this is one crazy-ass movie, the kind we rarely see in a theater these chicken-shit days with theatrical distribution as locked-down into studio monopolies as ever it was before the U.S. v. Paramount Pictures Supreme Court ruling. The ferocity of both the horror and the humor is delightful, punctuated by what is almost the most perverse use of a Fleetwood Mac tune in film history (I say "almost" because given the implications of where the movie might have been heading, given the revelation of one of the souvenirs Howard keeps in his living room, I must emphasize again that Kevin Smith chose to be a gentleman as a storyteller here—he could have and threatens to go much, much further than he does, and in that context the thrust of the titular 1979 Fleetwood Mac tune would have been a much raunchier feat). In fact, a close listening to Mac's "Tusk" lyrics provides yet another elegantly simple template for the narrative: "Why don't you ask him/if he's going to stay?/Why don't you ask him/if he's going away?/Why don't you tell me/what's going on?/Why don't you tell me/who's on the phone?" etc. to "Just tell me that you want me!"

I know, I know. I do go on.

Basically, it's all silly shit. This started and ended as another rude Kevin Smith joke, right?

I know I'm in a minority, but I was riveted and chilled by Smith's **RED STATE** (2011) and regretted not making the pilgrimage out to see it during its fleeting self-distributed theatrical run. Not making that mistake twice, I can only add that **TUSK**'s fond fearless fusion of horror and hilarity worked in spades for me. Structurally, there are certain similarities between the two films—the setup, the "dare", the trespass, the transgression, and Michael Parks' pivotal role—but these are superficial at best, save for the moral thrust (don't go where angels fear to tread, kids, for the consequences will be dire). **TUSK** is Kevin Smith's best film, in many ways. **TUSK** and **RED STATE** unexpectedly places Kevin Smith at the top of my short list of favorite contemporary genre filmmakers—even though it tanked, by mainstream barometers.

Many of my favorite creature features did, you know.

Like **FREAKED** and 2011's **CREATURE** (no, I'm not damning with faint praise: I championed **CREATURE** in 2011 and continue to[1], which may lose me any shred of credibility I may have for many), **TUSK** was declared an instant box-office bomb (earning in its first month $1.6 million, up against its reported $3.5 million budget). It was despised by many (Erik Lundegaard in The Seattle Times declared it "the most disgusting and pointless movie I've seen…I spent half the movie sick to my stomach," in his September 18th, 2014 review).

To which I say, again:

Fuck 'em if they can't take a joke.

©2014 Stephen R. Bissette
Special thanks for the initial heads up from Sean Morgan and for the road trip with Ian Richardson; I'm glad Sean and Ian alerted me to this in time! *Thanks,* guys!

[1] See for yourself in *Monster!* digest #2, Feb. 2014. *–ed.*

Dirty Uncle Jimbo's Top 10 Pumpkin Beer and Film Pairings for Halloween 2014

by James Bickert

Lately the Internet has been buzzing with pin-headed opinions on the orange tainted gourd elixirs flooding your neighborhood tap rooms. From Paste to Thrillist, annoying hipsters are pouring their highfalutin appraisals into our thirsty drinking holes. Let's face the facts. These Huffington Posters drink with one pinky out, comb their pubic like moustaches and pontificate their flaccid inebriated knowledge. Inexperienced wisdom that wouldn't even make a good cum-dumpster for violent prison sex. Opinions are as diverse as twats so here is another one to stink up your Halloween season. Unlike the rest of these scrubs, I refuse to rehash Beer Advocate for clicks. I've tried all the pumpkin beers on the market and I'm going to pair them with some films. I'm not talking a formal tasting of Paul Lynde's big dead gay taint in the proper glassware. I'm suggesting grabbing a 12-pack, putting in a film and riding that buzz to wino town. If you want to switch these beers out for a cheap American lager, than please do. If you want to switch the films out for a reach around...I ain't stopping you. In my educated opinion, beer and film should be about one thing only: a good time. When I develop a taste for Sauvignon Blanc, I'll share my pretentious Criterion Collection picks.

What the hell are my credentials? I sobered up from a blackout one day and had a wife, kid and an award-winning internationally distributed feature film. Don't remember any of it. After I finish this love letter, I'll see where the next blackout takes me. Now put that thumb back in your mouth and read.

10.
SCREAM BLOODY MURDER (1973)
New Holland Ichabod Ale
(New Holland Brewing Company)

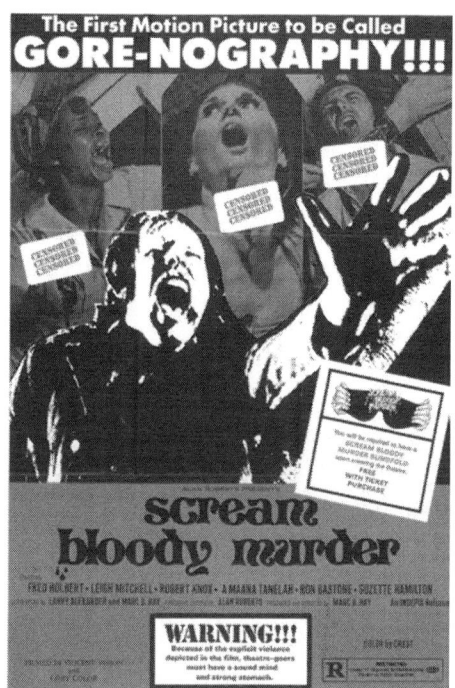

In an unconvincing tractor accident, a goofy kid accidentally dispatches his father and severs his stupid hand off. Years later, junior is released from a mental institution and embarks on a rampage of carnal killings with his sexy new hook. A poorly acted hoot with quotable dialogue, sleaze and gore to spare. I live for this kind of crud and writer/producer/director Marc B. Ray delivers an outstanding "stand-up and cheer" finale. Ripe for an improvisational shout-out party with your most demented friends—until the sacrilegious and incestuous undertones have you filling super-soakers full of hand sanitizer. I've paired **SCREAM BLOODY MURDER** with another limbless wonder, New Holland's Ichabod which depicts that famous headless horseman of legend on the label. Ichabod's malty goodness, packed with real pumpkin, sports delicate cinnamon and nutmeg notes that are sure to amplify your ride to this haunted grindhouse. **PHANTASM**'s (1979) Angus Scrimm shows up too!

9.
DEVIL IN MISS JONES 3: A NEW BEGINNING (1986) and DEVIL IN MISS JONES 4: THE FINAL OUTRAGE (1986)
Smuttynose Pumpkin Ale
(Smuttynose Brewing Company)

Hey, that is porn! Yeah, I know, but c'mon, it's Halloween! Fucking is one of the devil's favorite forms of artistic expression. If you want to truly warp-scare your mind this season, it's time to go all-in on some horrifyingly blasphemous smut. I prefer the shot-on-film stroke flicks of the '70s like Zebedy Colt's **THE DEVIL INSIDE HER** (1977—reviewed in *Weng's Chop* #6)—when Satan looked like King Diamond and sported a Milton Berle-sized cock. There was something magical about the loosey-goosey weirdness of hairy demonic orgies performed in the wilds of New Jersey. But I'm going to extended myself here. If you really want to go down the rabbit-hole into disturb-o-vision, then there actually is a video-lensed

8.
CONFESSIONS OF AN OPIUM EATER (1962)
Kentucky Pumpkin Barrel Ale (Alltech's Lexington Brewing and Distilling Co.)

It wouldn't be Halloween without an appearance from the maestro Vincent Price. I'm sure you've probably already exhausted his filmography, so here's an interesting little title many haven't seen. Recently released as part of the Warner Brother's Archive Collection on DVD, this fever dream action/adventure/horror hybrid is a real treat. Loosely based on the novel *Confessions of an English Opium-Eater* by Thomas De Quincey and sporting enough athletic action from Vinny, you wonder why he was never cast in a Bond flick! Price portrays a mercenary who descends into the tunnels under Chinatown to pull a **YOJIMBO** (1961)-style break-up of a female trafficking ring. Along his journey through this labyrinth, he takes periodic opium breaks to control his addictions. Like a pulp novel cover come to life, I've paired it with a manly and boozy ale. Kentucky pumpkins are thrown into the mash and aged in Kentucky bourbon casks to create a whopping 10% ABV potion. Perfect for this odd journey and one of the best tasting beers you will ever drink. Once you get nice and loopy, I recommend some comedic Price in **HIS KIND OF WOMAN** (1951)—co-starring with Robert Mitchum and Jane Russell.

production that does deliver a first class ticket. Director Gregory Dark literally puts Lois Ayres through hell in this perverted adaptation of *Dante's Inferno*. Parts 3 and 4 were shot in sequence so experience the moisture in one brave sitting. Shocking and entertaining as Hades itself, you're going to need something pleasant in your mouth to view all the slathered orifices being stuffed. I've chosen the clean and refreshing Smuttynose Pumpkin Ale. You'll appreciate how well-balanced this ale is compared to the unbalanced proceedings on screen. Stop being a whiny pussy and watch it already, geez.

7.
THE PIT (1981)
Pumpkin Fest (Terrapin Beer Company)

Maybe the weirdest film on this list. **THE PIT** features a 12-year-old autistic kid who discovers man-eating trolls living in a giant hole. After taking the advice of his teddy bear, our horny little lad lures the town to their demise. There is B-Horror gold in this pit and the fine folks over at Terrapin Brewing Company in Athens, GA have your poison. Despite the requisite spices, Pumpkin Fest is more akin to a

lager so purchase a 12-pack and toss back with some unnerving bone-headed originality. Low on blood but high on bizarre.

6.
HORROR RISES FROM THE TOMB
(*El espanto surge de la tumba*, 1973)
Warlock
(Southern Tier Brewing Company)

Paul Naschy (**WEREWOLF VS. THE VAMPIRE WOMEN** [*La noche de Walpurgis*, 1971]) escapes his usual full moon anguish to portray Alaric de Marnac, an executed warlock who returns to from the grave to exact revenge in this color-saturated (mostly red) atmospheric slice of greatness directed by Carlos Aured (**CURSE OF THE DEVIL** [*El retorno de Walpurgis*, 1973]). A film that contains everything you need from a Eurogore production—most notably the delicious international German bombshell, Helga Liné (**THE LORELEY'S GRASP** [*Las garras de Lorelei*, 1974]). We need an evil beer for this one, so I'm conjuring up Warlock. A dark and spicy imperial stout with cinnamon, licorice and pumpkin notes in one creamy well-carbonated (attached) head.

5.
SCARECROWS (1988)
Pumking (Southern Tier Brewing Company)

Here is a no-nonsense action/horror mash-up that doesn't bog it's britches in backstory. Paramilitary douchebags have pulled a heist and hijacked an air-

'80s horror film that delivers the goods with great performances and the right hair-raising tone. Be sure to get the unrated version so you can bathe in the extra violence and gore. **SCARECROWS** demand a ruler and Southern Tier's Pumking is the answer. Heavy on mashed pumpkin with a vanilla liqueur finish. Sorry to go back-to-back Southern Tier on you but this brewery knows what they're doing. If you feel cheated, go Weyerbacher, Unita or Cigar City. All good choices but you'll be back to bow.

4.
THE GRAPES OF DEATH
(*Les raisins de la mort*, 1978)
St-Ambroise Citrouille (The Great Pumpkin Ale) (McAuslan Brewing)

Most of us know French director Jean Rollin for his scantily clad and often surreal vampire flicks, but this underrated zombie film deserves some credit for sustaining an unsettling tone and delivering the *sauce tomate*. Since the film concerns the horrendous aftermath of pesticides sprayed on grapes, I've paired it with an outstanding French Canadian beer from Montreal. A light amber-colored ale with a slightly fruity finish that feels right at home amongst these rural vineyards of death.

plane. A double cross goes down with one of the thieves pulling a D.B. Cooper and parachuting with the stolen loot into a rural area full of satanic scarecrows. This is one of those rare instances of a late-

3.
KUNG FU FROM BEYOND THE GRAVE
(*Yin ji*, 1982)
Pumple Drumkin Spiced Ale

(Cisco Brewers Inc.)

Here is a film that can be best described as someone spiking your 8-ball with LSD. Insane and hysterically inept beyond repair. Sit back and let your jaw touch the floor as you watch our hero Billy Chong battle hopping vampires, zombies, a wizard… and even ol' Dracula himself gets in on the action. Toss in some menstruating prostitutes and you have yourself a real good time. Like the film, this tasty pumpkin pie beer has a little bit of everything. Just try to keep it from coming out your nose as you laugh in disbelief at the antics entering your seeing holes. Once you survive, try pronouncing the name of the 12-pack you just drank for an added comedy bonus. Why end the party? Make it a double-feature with **THE DRAGON LIVES AGAIN** (*Li san jiao wei zhen di yu men*, 1977). *SEE!* Bruce Lee befriend Popeye, The One-Armed Swordsman and Kwai Chang Caine from the TV show *Kung Fu* in Hell! *SEE!* Dracula, James Bond, Zatoichi, Clint Eastwood, The Godfather, The Exorcist, and Emmanuelle try to stage an underworld coup! *SEE!* One of the longest Kung-Fu fights against Mummies ever filmed! Yeah, you know you need to kill those pesky brain cells.

2.

UZUMAKI (2000)
Punkin Ale
(Dogfish Head Brewery)

A dark and disturbing film based on Junji Ito's manga serial, **UZUMAKI** is a phantasmagoric exercise in Lovecraftian-style horror overflowing with creepy Japanese flair. You can't fully understand **UZUMAKI**, and that is its strong point. A slow burn effectively illustrating with hair-raising precision that true terror is when we're helpless to comprehend what are minds are perceiving. **UZUMAKI** is sadly overlooked by genre fans in the modern age of Asian horror. Overshadowed by the hairdresser nightmares of **RINGU** (リング, 1998) and **JU-ON: THE GRUDGE** (呪怨じゅおん, 2002) which were more easily digestible into American remake consumption, I've chosen the Pumpkin beer

I.
ORGY OF THE DEAD (1965)
Shipyard Pumpkinhead Ale (Shipyard Brewing Co.)

Let us travel to a simpler time of classic monsters and heaving bosoms hot off the '60s burlesque circuit. You're going to need a case of beer for this rollick because we're going to view it all night long. Stephen C. Apostolof adapts an Ed Wood cocktail napkin (There was actually a novel!) and digs up Criswell's limp wrist for a circus sideshow guaranteed to make those slacks tight. Why Shipyard Pumpkinhead Ale? This is more of a vanilla-and-pumpkin-flavored cheap-assed American lager. Easy to funnel and ripe for your unhinged desires to gaze on the gams. Tits and spooks together like it was meant to be. Live it, love it, put **MONDO TOPLESS** (1966) on for a while and then play **ORGY OF THE DEAD** again. Hoot, holler and whistle. Hail Satan! Hail Titties! Hail Yeah! You get Bunny Glaser (**MOTEL CONFIDENTIAL** [1969]), Mickey Jines (**WILD GIRLS OF THE NAKED WEST** [1962]), Barbara Nordin (**MONDO KEYHOLE** [1966]), Lorali Hart, Rene De Beau, Fawn Silver and one of the hottest woman to ever scorch the planet: Pat Barrington (**AGONY OF LOVE** [1966]). Goddamn it, someone release a widescreen Blu-ray of this masterpiece! Now break a bottle over my head while I choke myself. This is living.

that built the number one brewery hell-bent on pushing the extremes of brewing. Dogfish Head Punkin' Ale. Consistently one of the best and always underrated by haters, this mildly hoppy dark ale with hints of brown sugar packs a 7% ABV that will enhance the slow creep inside your noggin'.

Super-swell ink-and-crayon sketch drawn by creator Jill Thompson in Tony's *Scary Godmother* book

AFTER THE GREAT PUMPKIN ENDS:
Lesser-Known Family-Friendly Halloween TV Treats

by Tony Strauss

Pumpkin carving night has always been an extra special part of the Halloween holiday season for me. Even more so than when I had my costume fully assembled and in-hand, Halloween time finally felt officially here once carving was underway. My family and I would, having already brought our carefully-selected pumpkin choices home, spread out double-layers of newspaper across the living room floor, break out the serrated steak knives and large spoons and carve and scoop to our hearts' content in front of the Halloweeniest things we could find on TV that night. In my younger days, I was always, whenever possible, keen to schedule carving night on whatever night they aired the iconic 1966 Peanuts special It's the Great Pumpkin, Charlie Brown—I say "whenever possible" because occasionally the show was aired too far before Halloween to make carving possible, as we lived in a warm enough climate to make premature carving a sure way to having a rotted-by-Halloween pumpkin on your front porch come trick-or-treating time. But that was only occasionally a problem, as the show usually tended to air less than a week before the actual holiday.

But in those olden days, aside from the aforementioned hallowed Peanuts classic holiday staple, there just wasn't much else in the way of TV Halloween specials to choose from—especially for me, given that we were in a fairly rural area and didn't get the option of being early cable TV subscribers. (Mind you, this was all well before The Simpsons were kind enough to start throwing horrific treehouses at us on a generously steady basis to ensure we had quality TV specials to carve our pumpkins by.)

Nowadays, being all middle-agey and without any kids of my own, I still have pretty much the same tradition (one might here say something about a refusal to grow up, but I'll throw a huge freaking tantrum if you do)...now it's sheet plastic instead of newspaper and a more elaborate array of carving tools, but the ritual is the same. A few days before Halloween the wife and I have carving night in front of the TV while it plays a bunch of family-friendly Halloween specials that I have over the years added to my annual ritual's entertainment. All October long in our house we watch horror films, going for the scariest terror-fests we can find, but on carving night I bust out the G-rated TV fare and we become giddy pumpkin-carving kids again. We can't go trick-or-treating without frightening parents and alarming neighbors, so this is how we, as boring non-party-animal adults, stay the youthful and vivacious shut-ins you see before you today. Laugh all you want. Pumpkin carving night *rocks*, and you only *wish* you could score an invite to ours.

Always, always, *always* kicking off the evening with *Great Pumpkin*, we sketch and carve and scoop all night in front of the boob tube like a couple dorky adolescents, and it's always fantastic. In addition to Charlie Brown and *The Simpsons*, there are a several other specials—both old and new—that have become part of the regular rotation for carving night, and since some of them are lesser-known or fairly forgotten, I figured I'd share a few of 'em with you *Chop*pers. Whether you have kids or not, these are some dang fun Halloween specials that appeal to the kid in everyone, and are well worth adding to your library to watch for your next big carving night!

Halloween is Grinch Night
October 29, 1977, USA. D: Gerald Baldwin
25 minutes

One autumn night down in Whoville, the ominous sour-sweet wind blows into town (yes, the very same wind that wakes up the Gree-Grumps in the tree stumps, whose angry growling runkles and grunkles up Punker's Pond, which disturbs the Hacken Cracks,

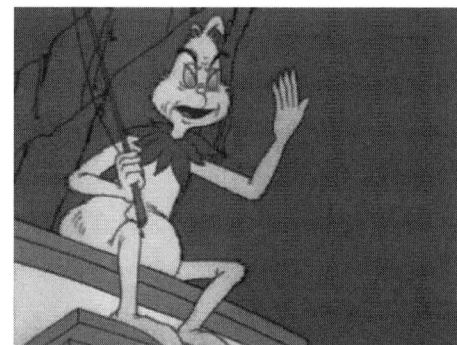

Top: The Grinch, riding his paraphernalia wagon, descends into Whoville. **Above:** Euchariah and Josiah sense the oncoming of the sour-sweet wind

who start a-yowling), and all the Whos in town lock their doors and throw their shutters, for they know what this runkling and grunkling and howling and yowling mean: it's going to be another Grinch Night.

Sure enough, high up on his mountain, the Grinch is plotting a trouble-making trip into town with the help of his long-suffering pooch, Max, who is ordered to load up the ginormous "paraphernalia wagon" then single-handedly pull the monstrosity with the Grinch riding astride it down towards the poor soon-to-be-terrorized Whos in Whoville. On his way down the mountain, he takes glee in crushing the flora and tormenting the fauna...even going so far as to hassling the poor Wuzzy WooZoo! The nerve of this guy!

Down in Whoville, a young Who named Euchariah (voiced by Gary Shapiro)—grandson of Josiah (Hal Smith) and Mariah (Irene Tedrow)—is forced to go outdoors for an emergency trip to "the cuphemism" to answer the call of nature. But nature has an even greater calling for him, it seems, because that sour-sweet wind blows him right out of his yard, up the mountain, and into the path of the descending Grinch! Now little Euchariah is literally the only thing standing between Whoville and Grinch Night! What's a Who to do?

Three *real* Halloween monsters out to make the most of the *Witch's Night Out*

This decade-later follow-up to the 1966 classic *How the Grinch Stole Christmas* doesn't really hold a candle to the original, either animation-wise, performance-wise, or plot-wise (especially plot-wise, because there's really no plot here...it's really all build-up that leads to nothing—like a Coldplay song). In lieu of a proper story, what we do get is a delightful bunch of weird Seussian characters and creatures saying funny words and singing catchy songs full of more funny words. And, of course, we get to revisit our favorite holiday crank, The Grinch himself (here voiced by narrator Hans Conreid, who, if you can't get Karloff again, is a pretty damn good second choice), and join him on a new plot to rain evil shenanigans down on Whoville.

Followed a few years later by 1982's *The Grinch Grinches the Cat in the Hat*, this is arguably the weakest of the three Grinch TV specials, but it is by no means one to pass by. For one thing, *it's a Grinch special made for Halloween!* Don't let the fact that the plot (such as it is) has absolutely nothing to do with Halloween—the holiday isn't even mentioned outside of the title—it's still a lot of goofy fun delivered in that whimsically surreal way that nobody did better than Dr. Seuss.

If you're going to get all scholarly and logical about its place within the Grinch TV special canon (which it appears I'm about to do), this makes more sense as a prequel to *How the Grinch Stole Christmas* based on plot details I won't spoil here (there are so few of them, after all), with the 1982 special being a much more logical-feeling follow-up to the 1966 original. Aside from a discontinuity of one secondary character, the trio flows pretty well in the 1977, 1966, 1982 viewing order.

But why am I thinking so deeply into this, when these were all pretty much made as standalone specials, and not as a multi-episode biography of the Grinch? I don't know...maybe I oughta lay off the Ken Burns for awhile. The point to be made here is that despite being of lesser caliber than the other two Grinch specials, *Halloween is Grinch Night* is still a whole lotta fun, and makes a totally solid addition to pumpkin carving night's viewing roster.

Witch's Night Out
October 27, 1978, Canada. D: John Leach
28 minutes

An orange boy named Small (voiced by Tony Molesworth) and a yellow girl named Tender ((Naomi Leach) are super excited about Halloween, walking through the neighborhood talking about how much they love the holiday, and how fun it is to dress up. Malicious the green lady (Catherine O'Hara) and Rotten the purple dude (Bob Church) come along and complain that they hate Halloween (they look to be the sort who pretty much hate everything...I mean, just check out their names!), when Goodly the mustachioed blue guy (director John Leach) overhears them, and posits that the problem with Halloween is it's just for kids. He then comes up with the inspired idea to plan a Halloween event that adults can enjoy. A friendly puffy pink woman named Nicely (Fiona Reid) thinks that a big Halloween bash is just the ticket, and the adults all come to a many-colored agreement (no, that's not a euphemism, you freakin' weirdo)—they decide to host it in "the old empty house on the edge of town". What could go wrong, right?

Well, wouldn't you know it: the supposedly empty house is occupied by a neurotic, no-longer-relevant witch (Gilda Radner), who is depressed by the lack of callers on Halloween nowadays. Just then, Goodly and Rotten wander in to check out the digs for tonight's big party. The witch overhears them, and becomes delighted by the news that she'll be hosting a party this evening!

Later that night while trick-or-treating, Small and Tender are disappointed that not only does everyone recognize them in their Halloween costumes, but rather than being frightened by their monstrous visages, everyone thinks they're *cute!* The shame! As the kids disappointedly tuck in for bed, Bazooey the shaggy red babysitter (Gerry Salsberg) reads them a story to cheer them up, about a fairy godmother that fixes everything. The kids feel they could've used a fairy godmother tonight, and wistfully wish that they could be real monsters so they could frighten people. Their wishes ring across the land into the ears of the witch ("Two engagements on the same evening!"), who rushes off from her now-in-full-swing house party to answer the call. Tonight, Halloween wishes will be granted, and the bejesus shall be scared out of many… the way things were meant to be on this special night!

Top: The spooky witch and her fluffy kitty.
Above: The townsfolk plan a Halloween event that's not "just for kids"

This 1978 Canadian obscurity is probably the least-known of this bunch, but it certainly doesn't deserve to be. Produced by (then-) husband and wife team of John Leach and Jean Rankin as a follow-up to their acclaimed 1974 special *The Gift of Winter*, this delightfully oddball Halloween tale is a breath of fresh animated air, displaying a unique design style that is a welcome and pleasant change from the more familiar cartoon traditions. With bold, solid-color characters and beautiful complimentary backgrounds, telling a well-written, wonderfully voiced holiday tale, it's a wonder this one never got more of a following. Simplistic and fun-spirited enough to please the kids while being clever and mischievous enough to entertain the grown-ups, this Canuck classic is well worth seeking out and adding to your family's Halloween roster. It's pretty easy to find, and comes at a reasonable price, plus the disc comes with a handful of bonus cartoons (as is frequently the tradition with these short run-time smaller-label releases) ranging from crap to cool, including the first Casper the Friendly Ghost short (1947), in which the death of a pet becomes cause for celebration!

Scary Godmother: Halloween Spooktacular

October 31, 2003, Canada. D: Ezekiel Norton
47 minutes

Obnoxious adolescent prankster Jimmy (voiced by Will Friedle) has been forced by his parents to take his younger cousin Hanna (Britt McKillip) out trick-or-treating with his friends: Katie (Britt Irvin), dressed as a cat; Daryl (Anthony Asbury), dressed as a giant piece of candy ("I figure when people see me, I'll make the candy they give out look small. So they'll overcompensate by giving us more!"); and Bert (Kevin Kleinbeirg), the professional baseball player in his fully-loaded cardboard SUV. Hannah's dressed as an

wants his friends to help him scare Hannah, so she'll run home and leave the older kids free to trick-or-treat without her slowing them down. In the name of candy, they all agree.

Jimmy tells Hannah she has to trick-or-treat "the spookhouse", a creepy abandoned house in the neighborhood where every Halloween, "the new kid" has to leave candy in the basement for the monsters that live there, or they'll get out and eat every kid in the world. When she goes into the dilapidated old house, they lock her in, and the poor girl begins crying in fear.

Naturally, this would be the perfect time for some sort of Scary Godmother to appear to help the poor child. Fortunately, that is exactly what happens.

Scary Godmother (Tabitha St. Germain) appears to comfort the child, explaining that monsters aren't anything to be afraid of…in fact, monsters are great! And to prove her point, Scary Godmother throws Hannah onto the back of her broom, and takes her to "The Fright Side", where Scary Godmother and all her monster friends live.

Needless to say, The Fright Side is a very Halloweeny place. In fact, Scary Godmother and her "broommate" Skully (Scott McNeil) the skeleton are preparing for their annual Halloween party, and they invite Hannah to attend.

adorable little princess ("Someday, I'll be a movie star/princess/veterinarian/astronaut/ballerina…with a pony!") who, as we learn via a fun "flashback" (actually an improvised re-enactment by the kids) is terrified of monsters, and has been given a flashlight from her parents to boost her confidence and protect her ("Monsters can't stand flashlights.") as she goes out on her trick-or-treating adventure.

They all meet up in the cemetery to plan out their candy-collecting route. Jimmy (dressed as a devil, natch)

Meanwhile, outside "the spookhouse", Jimmy and the kids wait for Hannah to come running out screaming …and wait…and wait. They're wasting valuable trick-or-treat time.

Back at the Fright Side, Hannah is having a blast, making all sorts of new friends: A family of vam-

A vampire family dispute at Scary Godmother's Halloween party

pires, Bug-A-Boo (Gary Chalk) the many-eyed furry monster, and Harry the werewolf (also Gary Chalk), who arrives and goes straight for the snacks while babbling on and on, so Scary Godmother interrupts with an easy recipe for the kids at home to make a snack to jam into the mouth of a babbling werewolf. Cute, fun stuff.

Hannah and her newfound friends from the Fright Side decide to turn the tables on the older kids, and devise a plan to go back to the spookhouse and deliver some scares that'll not only give 'em a Halloween trick they'll never forget, but teach them to show their younger friend a bit of respect.

I was already a fan of Scary Godmother before this ever got made, since I've long been a fan of writer/artist Jill Thompson through her great work in the comics medium. When the first *Scary Godmother* hardcover children's book came out in 1997, I snatched it right up and loved every page of it; when the Halloween special adapting the book was released in 2003, I did the same, finding it to be a delightfully faithful adaptation, capturing the humor and mischievous and whimsical holiday spirit of its source material perfectly.

This is one of those "family" specials that really earns its classification—this really *is* something the whole family can enjoy together. It's balances perfectly the silly more kid-centric stuff with clever, witty jokes that will appeal to the grown-ups. The jokes are consistently funny, the characters are well-defined and likable, and the monsters are a treat. There's really nothing here not to love. I guess if you wanted to really nitpick you could complain that the computer animation is a bit dated and video-gamey, but I find the animation has actually held up pretty well, due to its stylized, deliberately rough-around-the-edges, colorful and many-textured design. Had they gone for a slicker look, I think it would have fared far worse with age.

As it stands, this title carries my highest and heartiest recommendation for pumpkin carving night, or just general Halloween-time viewing for those looking for some family-friendly spooky-time fun. It's easy to find and cheap to buy, so just go grab it already… you'll thank me!

Scary Godmother: The Revenge of Jimmy

October 7, 2005, Canada/USA. D: Ezekiel Norton
44 minutes

Jimmy, now traumatized and horrified of monsters, has decided to boycott Halloween this year, and has rigged an elaborate monster trap in his bedroom, where he plans to safely hole up for the holiday. All his friends ignore him and proceed with their trick-or-

treating plans, of course. This infuriates Jimmy, so he decides to hatch a diabolical scheme to stop Halloween from coming.

To this end, Jimmy sneaks out at night to the pumpkin patch and goes on a kicking spree (giving him a sore foot that endures, often hilariously taking the piss out of his evil gloating). The other kids arrive the next morning to find every pumpkin with a big hole kicked in it. Since you can't have Halloween without pumpkins, the kids are devastated—Halloween is ruined. But not so fast! These big holes could just be the big mouths of the jack-o-lanterns! Hooray! Halloween is back on!

Or is it? Seems Jimmy isn't quite finished with his war on Halloween, and he's got a few more nasty tricks up his sourpuss' sleeve.

Meanwhile, over on the Fright Side, Scary Godmother is frantically preparing for the big Halloween bash, but strange things start happening. It seems that every time Jimmy strikes a blow against Halloween in our world, the Fright Side starts coming apart at the seams. As the inventive kids come up with solutions and fixes, the Fright Side is restored, but each new blow struck by Jimmy over in the land of the living causes successively more damage than those before. Will these poor kids with a really crappy friend and the burden of saving Halloween unfairly thrust upon their shoulders prevail? Egad, I hope so!

Scary Godmother: The Revenge of Jimmy is a wholly worthy follow-up to its predecessor, bringing the same mischievous sense of humor and Halloween fun back to the table for a new adventure with Scary

Godmother and the kids. Whereas the emphasis on the first special was on friendship and being accepted for who you are, the message this time around centers on using your imagination to make your own fun with whatever limited resources you may have. When the more commercialized and store-bought aspects of Halloween become unavailable to them, the kids have to get creative and create their own Halloween fun (in the process offering some cool do-it-yourself ideas, and a new snack recipe, t'boot), and hopefully it will inspire some of today's kids to do the same.

All the crazy characters from the first *SG* special are back—be they human, monster, or creatures of the night—and they're just as nutty and hilarious as we left them. Giving Jimmy the spotlight in the sequel was a great play; as his malicious scheming reaches more and more diabolical proportions, his evil sneer becomes more exaggerated and grotesque, eventually becoming a contorted mask of monstrosity, a physical manifestation of his evil deeds upon his face. You'll laugh in revulsion at how ugly this wicked little brat gets.

Once again filling its arsenal with jokes for both young and old, we get quite a few fun li'l pop culture references along the way; I noticed nods to **ALIENS** (1986), **STAR WARS** (1977), the *Dragon's Lair* video game, *How the Grinch Stole Christmas*, **THE WIZARD OF OZ** (1939)…even a clever tip-of-the-hat to **THE BIG LEBOWSKI** (1998). What can I say? You need to get this one, too…and you'll thank me yet again.

—

So there you have it, folks—some Halloween TV family fun that will neither give your kids nightmares nor send you grown-ups into a somnambulistic slumber of boredom. Hopefully some of you will be adding these to your own household viewing roster come next year's Halloween pumpkin carving night! Happy scoopin'!

—

Halloween is Grinch Night
1977, USA. D: GERALD BALDWIN
AVAILABLE FROM WARNER

Witch's Night Out
1978, CANADA. D: JOHN LEACH
AVAILABLE FROM MILL CREEK

Scary Godmother: Halloween Spooktacular
2003, CANADA. D: EZEKIEL NORTON
AVAILABLE FROM STAR/ANCHOR BAY

Scary Godmother: The Revenge of Jimmy
2005, CANADA/USA. D: EZEKIEL NORTON
AVAILABLE FROM ANCHOR BAY

Orson the vampire kid and his first living friend, Hannah

TERROR, TORTURE AND BEAUTY:
A NIKOS NIKOLAIDIS CAREER OVERVIEW

by Christos Mouroukis with Christoforos Theodorou

Not long ago I went to the movies with my fiancée Faye and my brother and we watched **DIRECTING HELL** *(Σκηνοθετώντας την Κόλαση / Skinothetontas tin Kolasi, 2011), a documentary by Christos Houliaras about legendary Greek director Νίκος Νικολαΐδης /Nikos Nikolaidis. It was well-made and it reminded me how much I like most of Nikolaidis' films. I decided that I wanted to write a career overview article on my favourite auteur, and* Weng's Chop *is the perfect vehicle for that.*

*Nikos Nikolaidis was born on the 25th of October 1939 in Athens, Greece. He published four books, directed several commercials, made a couple short films (*Lacrimae rerum *[1962] and* Anef oron *[1964]) which are considered lost, and nine feature films. He was considered part of N.E.K. (Neos Elinikos Kinimatografos, which means New Greek Cinema), but I refuse to consider his films as part of this particular "movement" because they are much more special. He died on the 5th of September 2007 in Athens, the city he always talked about through his work. ~CM*

Chapter One: The Films

EVRIDIKI BA 2037
(Ευριδίκη Βα 2037, a.k.a. **EURIDICE BA 2037**)
1975, Greece/West Germany

The title's girl Evridiki (Vera Tschechowa) is imprisoned in a basement where guys and girls bother her from the window above. She wants to escape, and there's something going on about a girl named Vera whom the audience never gets to meet, but I couldn't really follow the plot if there was any. Usually arthouse films are talk-fests, but this one is a silence-fest, as the actors rarely open their mouths to speak. This black-and-white oddity is the first feature film written and directed by Nikolaidis, and is the only one of the auteur's movies that I don't like (mainly because I don't get it).

According to the ancient Greek myth of Eurydice (wife of Orpheus, daughter of Apollo), when she died from a snake's bite and went to the underworld (world of the dead), Orpheus, who was madly in love with her, sang his very sad grieving songs and Adis (the God of the underworld) was so moved that allowed him to come to the underworld and take Eurydice

TA KOURELIA TRAGOUDANE AKOMA...:
Alkis Panagiotidis needs to hide a corpse, but this is the lesser of his problems.

Many critics claim that this film is an allegory for the seven-year (1967-74) dictatorship that took place in Greece and how people were completely suppressed and essentially isolated; however the film was shot in '75 and publicly screened five years later. Personally, I saw a "fear of the present and the future" situation, where the director tries to warn everyone that something is not going right, the human communication is gradually fading, the meanings of friendship and solidarity are lost, and the totalitarian regime is taking more and more control of our lives. This became even clearer to me when I watched some of his later films like **MORNING PATROL** (Πρωινή Περίπολος / *Proini Peripolos*, 1987) and **THE ZERO YEARS** (2005). (By the way, the fact that "BA 2037" was Nikolaidis' car plate number may suggest that the whole movie is a self-sarcastic game but at the same time an expression of deeply personal thoughts.)

The film won the award for "Debut Director" at the 1975 Film Festival of Thessaloniki and the director himself considered it his most solid work.

TA KOURELIA TRAGOUDANE AKOMA...

(Τα Κουρέλια Τραγουδούν Ακόμ / *"The Wretches Still Sing"*, a.k.a. **THE THRUSHES ARE STILL SINGING**)
1979, Greece

Back when there were still video stores in Greece I was browsing through some tapes and I found a copy of the original VHS release of this movie (complete with—surprisingly—English subtitles). It was an ultra-rare tape back then and this particular edition is still ultra-rare today. Needless to say, I bought it and still have it in my collection. Coincidentally, this is my favourite Nikos Nikolaidis film and one of the only three films that ever made me cry. (The other two are **THIS BOY'S LIFE** [1993] and **THE DEVIL'S REJECTS** [2005]. But I digress.)

The film takes place in a big house in which a failed drummer (Alkis Panagiotidis) carries around Vera's (Olia Lazaridou from **PARANGELIA!** [1980]) dead body and can't decide where to hide it, so he leaves it in the living room (this scene is hilarious). Soon one of his old buddies (Konstantinos Tzoumas from **O DRAKOULAS TON EXARHEION** [O Δράκουλας Των Εξαρχείων / *O Drakoulas ton Exarheion*, a.k.a. **DRACULA OF EXARCHEIA** [1983]; see *Monster! digest #2*) comes over for a pre-arranged reunion and they take funny pictures with the corpse.

The title's "wretches"[1] are joined by two more friends,

back to the world of the living under one condition: to walk in front of her and not look back to see her face until they reach the upper world. However, Orpheus was so thrilled and worried she might not be behind him that as soon as he put his feet on the ground of the living, he turned around to look at her, causing her sudden return to the underworld.

Nikos Nikolaidis' Eurydice (pronounced Evridiki in Greek) is trapped in a modern underworld (her apartment), labeled with the number "BA 2037", surrounded by forces that she cannot control, and fully submitted to the point of total passiveness. The modern Eurydice is so alienated and terrified that she doesn't let hope get in, or Orpheus to save her. She's a living dead woman, haunted by the ghost of herself and doomed to never-ending self-destruction. This claustrophobic atmosphere allows Nikolaidis to play with his own underworld obsessions: women vomiting, erotic interactions with little dolls and joyful play with bloody intestines, things that later became identity marks of his movies.

---

[1] The approximate English translation of the Greek title Τα κουρέλια τραγουδάμε ακόμα is "*The wretches still sing*"—the term "κουρέλια" is an older term for "rags" (when referring to clothing), which colloquially, when used to refer to people, most

played by Hristos Valavanidis (from **LOUFA KAI PARALLAGI** [Λούφα και Παραλλαγή, a.k.a. **LOAF AND CAMOUFLAGE**, 1984]) and Rita Bensousan, who is dressed as Batgirl. They have many stories to tell, all of them abstract and philosophical. But soon enough the guys will gang-rape the girl, who the next day doesn't seem to mind anymore. After all, she says, she's been doing sexual favours for them in the past. The wretches wake up one morning in the middle of naked bodies of strangers, apparently there after a huge party. A girl may be or may not be dead. They never find the body…"Vera is the name of an age that has been lost forever".

I haven't seen such gorgeous cinematography on any other '70s film from Greece. Rock n roll, nostalgia for the '50s and the '60s, remorse for their critical life choices, suicidal tendencies, and loss of hope for the future might be well-known in the American cinema, but for Greek film production standards, **THE THRUSHES** fell like a bomb from nowhere. Due to its unusual subject and approach, it made many people love it madly while many others totally hated it. Even the film critics, who up to then were more or less on the same page regarding which films were giving an *avant-garde* direction to Greek cinema, were divided into supporters and opponents. Undoubtedly it is a film that shook many people of all ages and many generations. Even now, 35 years later, young people keep being inspired and influenced by this timeless film. It may be the absolute definition of a Greek cult film.

The use of music in the movie is also unique:

---

closely approximates "wretches" in English. *–ed.*

Panagiotidis is also a drummer in real life and there is an amazing scene where he's jazz-jamming with a flute player while he is narrating the story from his teens when he met Vera, the woman who haunted him forever, his unfulfilled love…a true obsession. We've never seen this kind of storytelling in any other film globally.

According to Nikolaidis, **TA KOURELIA TRAGOUDANE AKOMI…** is an effort to give voice to the '50s generation, who was muzzled and suppressed, leading it to disappointment and decadence. I still remember the first time I watched the film when I was 19 years old, what a great shock it was to discover that there were young people back in the '50s and '60s in Greece dancing to the rhythms of Little Richard and Elvis, flirting and fucking around like bunnies, committing little crimes as gangs, making music bands, going to demonstrations, watching *film noir* and reading poetry! Without watching this movie, one is probably unconsciously carrying the somehow dominant opinion that the '50s in Greece were the post-civil-war era full of hope, social peace and funny, relaxing movies.

GLYKIA SYMMORIA
(Γλυκιά Συμμορία a.k.a. **SWEET BUNCH**)
1983, Greece

"Then go to hell!"
"That's where I came from."

A bunch of outlaw romantic anarchists (with poetic tendencies) get involved with pornography, money, murder and some degenerates. Soon their house will be surrounded by armed fascists. Or maybe I'm not

GLYKIA SYMMORIA: Making porn was once a practical method of revolution.

GLYKIA SYMMORIA

reading this film properly. It doesn't matter; it's a masterpiece and it's the only Greek film that made it into my list of 125 genre films of my *Cult Films* book, published in Greece by Michalis Sideris.

PROINI PERIPOLOS

Argiris, the main protagonist (played by Takis Moshos) is a cool guy in his thirties who is staying with Marina (Dora Masklavanou), a young and troubled woman, in a big house that belongs to Sofia (Despoina Tomazani). Sofia is a 35-year old woman who has illegal connections to a rebel organization, but tries to keep the others uninvolved. The three of them have formed some kind of commune/gang and manage to make their living by robbing supermarkets, starring in porn movies, fooling restaurant owners or even satisfying necrophiliac rich men's fantasies. Andreas (Takis Spiridakis), the fourth member of the sweet bunch, is released from the prison where he was, it is implied, imprisoned for political reasons. He joins the others and quickly we find out that Sofia is not directly connected to them, but only through her recently killed boyfriend, whom they always mention, showing how much they miss him. Despite the tension between them, it becomes clear that they are, above anything else, in solidarity with each other, showing a unique sense of friendship.

While organizing a big robbery (which will lead to a very funny death), an undercover cop (Alkis Panagiotidis) is constantly in front of their house, spying on them and making them feel violated. The tension increases, one thing leads to another and quickly they realize they have reached the point of no return. It is then that they decide to fight for their right of self-determination, and that's the key point of the movie. This bunch is sweet not only because they're just "tea-leaves" and not criminals with guns, but also due to their unconditional solidarity and sense of dignity. All of the above takes place under the mesmerising tones of Giorgos Hatzinasios' score, whose music became one of the first—maybe the first ever—Greek film O.S.T. that came out as an album.

Nikolaidis was a huge fan of the classic American cinema, and we don't think there has been a better example of an American-influenced Greek film than this. However, there's something purely "Nikolaidish" here, containing some moral elements not very common in the American films. One of Nikolaidis' favourite directors was Sam Pekinpah, director of **THE WILD BUNCH** (1969) and **STRAW DOGS** (1971), and it is more than evident that the film under review is also a homage to **THE WILD BUNCH**, where the members of the gang live and die like they have absolutely nothing to lose, and only according to their own rules. It seems that Nikolaidis wanted to keep these characteristics in his gang, while filtering out the unjustified violence and killings, in order to create a bunch of his own morality and ideology, thus baptised "sweet". Nikos Nikolaidis strongly believes in friendship, love, self-determination and personal freedom, and most of his films are hymns to these values.

The movie received many awards in Greece, and the Greek Cinema Critics Union has voted it as one of the ten most important movies in the history of Greek film. It was also a huge commercial success, as the number of the tickets reached the amount sold for Francis Ford Coppola's **APOCALYPSE NOW** (1979), which was screened the same year.

PROINI PERIPOLOS
(Πρωινή Περίπολος, a.k.a. **MORNING PATROL**)
1987, Greece

MORNING PATROL (that's the English title) stars Michele Valley (also the star of 1990's **SINGAPORE SLING** and 2005's **THE ZERO YEARS**), and she's walking around in a destroyed, post-nuke Athens. She is trying to pass through the forbidden zone and reach the sea but the Morning Patrol is watching her and there are traps everywhere. She seems to be (almost) alone and tends to get a bit philosophical. Somebody attacks her and she slaughters him with a knife. She goes into a house and the TV is still on, playing a Frank Sinatra film (that I could not identify) and then **THE BIG COMBO** (1955). She goes to a theatre and watches a film until she is again attacked. Soon a Patrol Guard will join her (Takis Spiridakis from **GLYKIA SYMMORIA** [1983]). What does all that have to do with pills, guns, and the government? **PROINI PERIPOLOS** (1987) is one of the very few Greek sci-fi films and arguably the best, mainly due to the gorgeous cinematography by Dinos Katsouridis and the scenography of Marie-Louise Vartholomaiou (the director's wife).

Here, Nikolaidis returns back to the paths of his first film, **EVRIDIKI BA 2037**: trapped people, loneliness, unknown future, broken communication, hopeless escape efforts. Now instead of an apartment, we see a whole town guarded by the system, an infinite war-zone suggesting that a war has at some point begun but never ended. In our opinion, the atmosphere of this film is by far the most haunting in all history of Greek cinema.

But the biggest shock for us was the answer Nikolaidis gave when everyone asked him where the hell he fond these places and how did he set them up. He simply responded: "It was all shot in Athens, in streets that we walk every day". Some might say this proves that he is a director with the rare ability of changing something already existing into something unreal or adjusting his vision to what his economic budget allows. But we think that there's more to it than that. The total control over people's thought, the loss of values like friendship, love or freedom are not his fears about a dark and faraway future, but his worries for the present, the life as we live it. Shooting a post-nuke film in the streets of today's Athens is a direct way for him to manifest his perception of today's rotten human relationships and the dominance of the state fascism.

In an interview some years before he died, when he was asked to comment on his film **PROINI PERIPOLOS**, Nikolaidis stated that even 15 years after the film came out, he was really frightened of it and terrified by the idea of watching it again. He

PROINI PERIPOLOS:
Blasting shotguns against authority

SINGAPORE SLING: The eroticism of the dead through the lens of Greece's greatest celluloid poet

felt like everything he was scared of and all of his fears expressed in the movie eventually came true and we're now living the world of the Morning Patrol: ice in human relationships, silence, and triumph of the state fascism…silence and death everywhere.

PROINI PERIPOLOS received the awards of best Direction, Scenography and Direction of photography in the 1987 Thessaloniki Film Festival and was selected to be screened in two international film festivals in Portugal and France. It's a shame that Giorgos Hatzinasios was not awarded for the atmosphere he created with his music.

SINGAPORE SLING: O ANTHROPOS POU AGAPISE ENA PTOMA

(*Singapore Sling:* Ο Άνθρωπος που Αγάπησε ένα Πτώμα a.k.a. **SINGAPORE SLING**)[2]
1990, Greece

Please allow us to quote some of Christos' band's lyrics:

"So I'm stepping in the dungeon, I'm surrounded by masks, every other instrument that you can imagine".
- "Only the Night" by The Nosferatu Dot

In this neo-*noir* (with the gorgeous black-and-white cinematography by Aris Stavrou), two women (Meredyth Herold and her mother Michele Valley) stab a man five times and then bury him alive in their garden, showing great deal of enjoyment while doing so. Soon they entrap another wounded man named Singapore Sling (Panos Thanassoulis) and torment him until the end of the picture. He was found there because he was obsessively looking for a girl named Laura.

This was indented to be a black comedy, but with so much sadomasochism, lesbianism, incest, paedophilia, water-sports, vomit, alcoholism, guns, and instruments of torture, it really seems very gruesome to laugh with. It is Nikos Nikolaidis' most famous film outside Greece, mainly because it managed to break art-house boundaries and enter genre territory. It is very decadent and you will undoubtedly enjoy it very much.

There is not much to say really for this very special film, mainly because the experience of watching it is just indescribable. There is something really disturbing going on that is at the same time inexplicably funny. For the Greece of 1990 this movie was like a bomb on the head of conservatism. It is clear that Nikolaidis is trying to provoke everyone, but it is also obvious that he is really enjoying it. His exact words when asked to comment on it were: "With **SINGAPORE SLING**, I had the impression I was shooting a comedy with elements from the Ancient Greek Tragedy… Later, when some European and American critics characterized it as *one of the most disturbing films ever shot*, I started to believe that something is going wrong with me. Later, when the British censorship forbid it's screening, I started to believe that finally something is going wrong with every one of us."

---

[2] Not to be confused with the 1999 DTV Rena Riffel/Shannon Tweed boobfest **SINGAPORE SLING**, directed by genre mainstay thespian James Hong (**BLADE RUNNER** [1982], **BIG TROUBLE IN LITTLE CHINA** [1986]). –ed.

People looking for a deeper meaning or a reason behind all the vomit, the incest, the violence and the unstoppable orgasmic deliriums will be disappointed. Nikolaidis takes all the kinds of cinematic alcohol he loves (*film noir*, lesbianism, grave digging, S&M outfits, the sound of the rain, women alone in big houses), puts it all together, and tries to get us drunk with his special cocktail. He's having a party and he's enjoying it. There's nothing more to it than that and there never was. He indeed once said that he never thought before making a movie, "I want to show this or that" or "I want to pass this message", etc. He was like a little kid having fun, playing with his toys. If you're not willing to join the game, don't bother watching his movies. But in case you do, be careful: one moment you might pee on yourself laughing and the next moment you may wanna kill yourself. But that's life, right?

TO KORITSI ME TIS VALITSES
(Το Κοριτσι Με Τισ Βαλίτσεσ, a.k.a. **GIRL WITH THE SUITCASES**)
1994, Greece

The **GIRL WITH THE SUITCASES** (this is the English title) is played by sensual Meredyth Herold. She is looking for her friend Takis in his apartment but instead he finds Michalis (Lakis Lazopoulos), who is there to feed the fish and take care of the plants while the tenant is away. He doesn't speak English and she doesn't speak Greek, but nevertheless they fall in love.

This is the only TV movie by director Nikos Nikolaidis, and I can't understand how the deal was possibly made between him (an anti-establishment director) and the network (ANT1, a very mainstream channel). It was probably broadcast only once and it's the auteur's sole feature-length film not available on DVD. The quality of the copy I found on YouTube (complete with some of the original commercials) is shit and the sound is rarely in sync.

Regardless of how much humour there is in Nikolaidis' work, this is his only true comedy, but still not very proper for television, especially if you consider that it was made 20 years ago. It's also the only film of his that I hadn't seen before writing this article. Unfortunately, while not bad, it never really takes off, though the scene in which Michalis talks about his sad and lonely past is quite touching.

Lakis Lazopoulos is a really famous comedian in Greece whose satire TV shows do record ratings. He followed in the footsteps of the more mainstream Harry Klynn and the more radical Tzimis Panousis, and also maintains a great film career with starring roles in movies such as **O KALYTEROS MOU FILOS** (Ο Καλύτερος Μου Φίλος, a.k.a. **MY BEST FRIEND**, 2001) and **FOVOU TOUS ELLINES...**

English language poster art for **THA SE DO STIN KOLASI, AGAPI MOU**

97

SEE YOU IN HELL, MY DARLING

(Φοβού τους Έλληνες!, a.k.a. **BEWARE OF GREEKS BEARING GUNS**, 2000).

THA SE DO STIN KOLASI, AGAPI MOU

(Θα σε Δω στην Κόλαση Αγάπη μου, a.k.a. **SEE YOU IN HELL, MY DARLING**)
1999, Greece

"You don't wear panties!"
"I never wear panties."

This film revolves around an armed robbery, but it is really about alcoholism, chain-smoking, neurosis, murder, deadly accidents, violence, asphyxiation, gorgeous women, lesbianism, and sex.

This is the first film from Nikos Nikolaidis I ever heard about, back in '99. The (surprisingly mostly favourable) reviews described it as something unusual for a Greek film and I was intrigued to see it, but I couldn't find a theatre that'd screen it. I bought it on DVD when it came out and I was astonished, mainly due to its sexuality. Unlike the majority of Greek films from the era this one features incredibly professional sound design and cinematography. Unfortunately though, the editing goes back and forth, which is a technique I find annoying.

Nine years after **SINGAPORE SLING**, this movie came like a light sequel, since here also one can find the *film noir* influence and the triangle of two women, and one man trying to kill one another in a big house. The three of them have organized an armed robbery together, but the erotic attraction between all three is messing things up. The sudden loss of trust creates hate and anger, followed by a strange urge to fuck.

Nikolaidis puts the concept of the erotic triangle to trial, and the result is a provocative flirt with death. The colors are amazing, but a colorful *Noir* loses a bit of its atmosphere. The hilariously disturbing images of **SINGAPORE SLING** are missing here, however there is a series of incredible punchlines between the two women, as if they were playing in a David Lynch film. Through the lens of Nikolaidis, murder becomes a little game of hide-and-seek.

Unfortunately, for the first time since 1975, a Nikolaidis film didn't receive any awards at all, and it wasn't even screened in any theater, officially showing the disappointment of the critics and the audience, mainly due to the fact that, after **SINGAPORE SLING**, it became clear to everyone that Nikolaidis was using cinema as his hobby and had converted the *style* of the movie to its main reason of existence. It was like giving him a message of, "Okay, you played your little game with **SINGAPORE SLING**, now get serious!" He seemed like a perfectionist, but only in the directing. His stories were no longer interesting or inspiring, a fact that made some critics who up to then were huge admirers wonder why he didn't start to direct the screenplays of others. Because it was his hobby! He didn't care if people or critics found his films interesting or not. His main purpose was to entertain himself, and if by that, some people were also entertained, it was even better.

O HAMENOS TA PAIRNEI OLA

O HAMENOS TA PAIRNEI OLA

(Ο Χαμένος τα Παίρνει Όλα, a.k.a. **THE LOSER TAKES ALL**)
2002, Greece

"I don't understand you."
"I don't understand me either."

A man without a name (Giannis Angelakas) is looking for a place to stay. Some prostitutes find him a couch.

He is hassled by the police, but he just makes fun of the dirty cops. Soon he meets a young musician (Simeon Nikolaidis) and the gorgeous Melissa (Ioanna Pappa). Everyone is into chain smoking and alcohol, and occasionally some drugs…and apparently everyone is fucking everyone. Additionally, everybody seems to be very philosophical; even Sid Vicious' version of "My Way" gets quoted.

Anyway, the protagonists get a "job" through the underworld. They have to deliver a gun, some bullets and a couple bags of drugs. They rip-off the other guys (and even get a hostage), so they get an even bigger "job". They arrange a rip-off again. Will they make it alive and with the money in the bag or will they die trying?

This is a very engaging film if you've ever felt like an outcast. It is the first film of Nikos Nikolaidis that I saw in a theatre and I was amazed. Whilst watching it again (for the purpose of writing this article) I asked my friend Ilias if such a world exists in real life, and he said apparently not. Nikos Nikolaidis humour here is contagious, as when the film is finished you want to somehow start talking like its characters. It is quite touching, too, because you feel for the heroes. My favourite scene is the bust: the police attack a rave party and Angelakas pretends he's a cop and saves Simeon Nikolaidis' ass.

The promotion for this film was quite unique, as when it first came out you could see graffiti with the movie's logo everywhere in Central Athens. Greece's capital is full of street art so this approach was somehow popular with young audiences.

Giannis Angelakas is a living (somehow anti-authoritarian) legend in Greece; arguably the biggest rock star, he is considered a poet (with his lyrics always having multiple layers of meanings) and his books are praised by intellectuals.

Greece, with a population of only 11 million, is really a small place; I [Christos] have seen Giannis Angelakas' previous band Trypes live when I was young, and Faye tells me that she spotted Ioanna Pappa in a cafe in Athens' Exarchia area. Also, Fotis Mitsis who was the Steadicam operator in **THE LOSER TAKES ALL** was also the cinematographer of my first feature-length film, **COSTAS THE BARBERIAN** (2006) which is the only film I directed never to be screened anywhere.

THE ZERO YEARS
2005, Greece

Two men (whom we never see) may or may not be watching a seedy whorehouse (because the CCTV cameras are dead), in which the beautiful-but-desexed

prostitutes torture and humiliate the masochistic clients in the basement. A client will soon disappear and the interrogations will start. Well, not really soon, as we have to wait for ages for the movie to take off. Other than that, expect the usual chain-smoking and lesbianism from a Nikos Nikolaidis movie along with needles, violence, and binocular surveillance.

This is the last Nikos Nikolaidis film, and it is the closest he ever got back to his roots and to **EVRIDIKI BA 2037** in particular, so in a sense you could say that his filmography came full circle. It is also his only theatrical film not to be shot on film but on video instead, and unfortunately it shows.

In **THE ZERO YEARS** it is like all the ideas of the previous Nikolaidis films are meeting each other: the isolation and alienation of **EVRIDIKI BA 2037**, the gang feeling and the fight for dignity of **TA KOURELIA TRAGOUDANE AKOMI, GLYKIA SYMMORIA** and **O HAMENOS TA PAIRNEI OLA**, the post-apocalyptic world and the dream to escape towards the sea of **PROINI PERIPOLOS**, as well as the perversion and orgasmic darkness of **SINGAPORE SLING** and **THA SE DO STIN KOLASI AGAPI MOU**.

But putting all your obsessions and great ideas together won't necessarily give an awesome result that sums up all of your original and innovative thoughts. It might as well produce an image that shows repetition, self-involvement, neutered obsession, a lack of inspiration, and in a way, conservatism. Nevertheless, the film raises very serious questions about the things that torture the director's mind, such as thought control, fear of the unknown, state terrorism, dominance and submission, women's relationship to birth and friendship. Although it lacks a lot of his previous perfectionism in terms of photography, sound and atmosphere, someone that has never watched any other Nikolaidis film might find **THE ZERO YEARS** a true revelation.

We had the luck of being present when the film was presented in the 2005 Thessaloniki International Film Festival, and Nikos Nikolaidis was there to answer the audience questions. He was also asked to say something to the audience before the film started and he only said the following words: "The film is not talking about some distant future, it is about today's world and this is how it should be read.", confirming for one more time that his films show the nightmare of the bizarre and cruel world we live in, as he is experiencing it.

"One thing is certain: You will not be entertained".
-Nikos Nikolaidis

Chapter Two: The Books

Nikos Nikolaidis was the screenwriter of all of his films, showing that he was not only a talented director but also a great storyteller. In fact, not a lot of people know that he started off as a writer, and not as a filmmaker, and that he continued writing books until the day he died.

His first book, *Oi tymvoryhoi* (English title: *The Grave Diggers*), which was published in 1966, was a collection of stories, written in the period 1962-1965, when Nikolaidis was still in his early twenties! Reading the book, it is quite a shock when you realize that all the fears described in the films he shot later, like **EVRIDIKI BA2037** and **MORNING PATROL**, were already torturing him. In all the stories of *Oi tymvoryhoi*, one can feel the presence of a state of terror, controlling everything and people feeling alienated and constrained. For someone who knows the Greek history of the '50s and '60s only from the school books will definitely not understand how the writer perceives reality. The truth is that from 1949 when the Greek Civil War was over until 1967 after a military coup, the army established a dictatorship where there was a totalitarian control of every aspect of life; the everyday life in Athens was already in a climate of terror against anything progressive, from political ideas to rock 'n' roll. Even government laws were written to restrain how people dressed or cut their hair.

In that era's Greece, it was revolutionary for a young man just to go to the billiards hall or the rock 'n' roll club to dance; to read poetry or to ride a motorcycle. This is the world in which Nikos Nikolaidis grew up and the other three books that he wrote are full of stories from a youth that he seems to be missing a lot of, even a youth that he would like to have lived.

Between shooting **EVRIDIKI BA 2037** (1975) and **TA KOURELIA TRAGOUDANE AKOMI** (1978), Nikolaidis wrote a screenplay for a movie (and what a movie would that be!), but he couldn't find the funding to shoot it—no producer would take that risk. So he decided to publish it in 1977 as a novel called *Orgismenos Valkanios* (English title: *The Angry Balkan*). It was—like his movies—a shock for the traditional Greek literature, since it featured a young rebel boy as the main character, living stories full of little crimes, sex and violence, motorcycles and billiards, all taking place in the Greece of the '50s and '60s, the same period for which **TA KOURELIA TRAGOUDANE AKOMI** works as full nostalgia. Many claim that if this book had succeeded in becoming a movie, it would probably be his best. There is a funny line from the book that is often quoted when someone is talking about Nikolaidis and his perception of the place he grew up: "This country is the most irregular verb in the whole world."

Between 1977 and 1993 he didn't publish any books, but he did publish the screenplays of **TA KOURELIA TRAGOUDANE AKOMI** and **GLYKIA SYMMORIA**. His influence from the American films of James Dean and Marlon Brando is so deep that even 15 years after the novel *Orgismenos Valkanios* and the movie **TA KOURELIA TRAGOUDANE AKOMI**, in 1993, he wrote a new book titled *Gourounia ston anemo* (English title: *Pigs in the Wind*), with the same atmosphere as *Orgismenos Valkanios* and apparently the same character, but around his thirties. The story revolves around the days of Christmas, as many "Nikolaidish" stories, and it is full of references to old American films with Kim Novak (his personal favorite actress) and Humphrey Bogart. In fact, the novel is a direct reference to Bogart's movie **DARK PASSAGE** (1947)—the main hero is trying to escape to a faraway place to get away from what is hunting him, in this case the dead body of his father in the bathroom.

The same atmosphere and similar series of events take place in his last novel, *Mia stekia sto mati tou Montezuma*, which he wrote right before he died and which was published in 2007, just after his death. However, here his style is more mature and complete than ever and although we see the same characters as in *Gourounia ston anemo*, it seems like he has lived all these stories himself, in his real life. His writing is completely unique for the Greek standards; nevertheless one can also feel the narrative voice of Jack Kerouac and the perverted descriptions of Charles Bukowski.

Chapter Three: The TV ads

Somewhere back in the '80s and '90s in Greece, when we were little kids (well, at least half of us), we were watching TV like crazy. It was a period when things on Greek TV were not yet so much under control, there were really funny or "qualitative" TV series and many, many cartoon series and even anime movies! And there was a strange thing going on that our parents didn't quite get: we were still stuck in front of the TV screen, even during the commercial breaks. You see, most TV ads back then had a small story to tell—most of the times funny—and were shot with lots of talent and professionalism.

In fact there was a group of ads that was quite special, because you felt they were advertisements shot in the US for American products. We were entering another world, unknown to us through these short clips: sexy women, swing, rock 'n' roll, jazz, surfing, motorcycling, leather jackets, smoke, shadows and old Cadillacs... Well, after a lot of years, we discovered that all of these specific style TV ads (seriously, *all* of them) were made by Nikos Nikolaidis!

Beers, ice creams, chocolate milks, cleaning papers, sports shoes, super markets, banks, shampoos, camera film, snacks, deserts, newspapers, coffee, chewing gums and alcohol liquors...he's done all of it! And it is quite obvious that he had so much fun doing them. Often he would apply the *film noir* atmosphere, or the American college/surf-party style. Then again, if he couldn't put in some shadows, some hard nipples or some Cadillac, he would present new, unexpected images; many of these images became iconic, leading to their place as a bizarre part of Greek cult television history.

Chapter One reviews by Christos Mouroukis with Christoforos Theodorou
Chapters Two and Three by Christoforos Theodorou

Greek DVD collection of Nikos Nikolaidis's films

THE WILDSIDE/KRONOS UNIVERSE IS NOW

PollyGrind V
AWARD WINNER

ADVOCATE OF A DIFFERENT BREED:
WENG'S CHOP

AWARD WINNING!!

www.wengschopstore.com

STEVE'S VIDEO STORE OF DOOM: HALLOWEEN SPECIAL - CANDY AND TV AND THE CRAZY MEMORIES OF THE '70S AND '80S

by Steven Ronquillo

Another year, another fear here at Steve's Video Store. As a look at the kids coming in for candy and the adults for the movies of their choice, I can't help but think back to my days as a kid (like I always do, as I'm officially an old fart this year). So for this Halloween frightfest I look back to the olden days of TV when Halloween was a bigger holiday than it was today. And I'm not disparaging today—it's a bigger holiday with the masses now than in my day, and the TV shows today are the stuff we wish we had back then. But the ones I'm going to be talking about were wackier and had an insane anything-goes edge we rarely see today besides batshit crazy shows like Penny Dreadful *and* American Horror Story. *But let's go back to the '70s and see what we can dig up!*

THE FAT ALBERT HALLOWEEN SPECIAL
(1977)

In this little gem we see fat Albert and the gang going out for Halloween and finding out that just because a person looks scary to you doesn't mean they're not nice. In this modern era of stranger danger and stupid paranoia this wouldn't fly today. But this is a sweet innocent cartoon from a sweet innocent time, and I love how when the one kid fucks around and just behaves like an ass his dad comes looking for him and gives him the "when I get you home your ass is grass and I'm the mower" look. I can remember the old ladies like the ones in this special who would go all-out on Halloween to give us amazing homemade treats so they could see "their kids" as they called them.

Mine was Mama Morton—she made popcorn balls as big as softballs and the best damn homemade popcorn you ever ate. She would have to know every one of us by name so she would know who "her kids" were. She lived for Halloween and always had to make sure her kids got there treats. It was a sad day when we found out she passed on, but it was sort of a good thing she left when she did, because not even a year after she died was when they put the unofficial ban on homemade treats. I will always love ya, Mama Morton... from your shy little boy named Steve.

THE PAUL LYNDE HALLOWEEN SPECIAL
(1976)

Paul Lynde was a gay comedian from the '70s whose gimmick was that he was a flamingly flamboyant gay caricature (only a slight stretch). Sid and Marty Krofft were the kings of one-show extravaganzas like this; all of them were tacky and weird but we loved them to death. This one has been a cult hit because it was the first TV appearance of Kiss! Where else are you going to see a flaming gay man, Witchiepoo (Billie Hayes) and one of the best rock bands ever rubbing elbows!

Kiss This! The phenomenally popular glam rockers made their small screen debut in *The Paul Lynde Halloween Special*.

THRILLS, CHILLS AND LAUGHS!

Special. What better place to spend Halloween than in a haunted house with Paul Lynde? Guests include Tim Conway, Florence Henderson and Kiss.

THE PAUL LYNDE HALLOWEEN SPECIAL

abc **7:00**

Lawd have mercy, is this the most '70s fun you can have!

The Halloween I first saw this was a night my mom and dad dropped me and my sis and her friend Kim off at my grandmother's. We had just gotten back from trick or treating and had some candy. So my sis and Kim were watching this and then Kiss' song "King of the Night Time World" came on and my grandmother said, "Uh, *NO!*" They got sad, I laughed, but everyone went to bed so it was me and my candy as I waited for midnight and **THE ABOMINABLE DR. PHIBES** (1971) on *The Unknown Zone*. WOO-HOO!

DARK NIGHT OF THE SCARECROW
(1981)

I think this was the last Halloween I trick-or-treated, but I went up my grandmother as my sis had already retired and was out with her friend Kim. So I was at my grandma's, and yes, I was still a coward, but *It's the Great Pumpkin, Charlie Brown* (1966) was going off and I was still in a Halloween mood. So then a trailer for this came on and for some reason it hooked me and my grandma.

Good god, did this one blow me away! One part Revenge Thriller, one part Slasher, and all parts awesome. This was an amazing little movie which gladly holds up today. It's about a little girl named Marylee (Tonya Crowe) who hangs around with a mentally handicapped man named Bubba (Larry Drake) who, when she is mauled by a dog, is accused of diddling her by Otis Hazelrigg (Charles Durning), the leader of the town assholes (who himself wants to diddle the little girl). So he gets his band of assholes to find him and they accidentally murder him, so they cover up their crime. But some guy or thing in a scarecrow suit (like the one they killed Bubba in) comes after them.

What makes this one stick out is there isn't one iota of sympathy for the assholes getting killed, so you can sit back and enjoy their deaths. And even better, there is no resolving of the issue of who is behind the mask, which I like. This was one of the last gasps of '70s TV horror movies in both style and ambiguity.

My grandmother and I really liked it; even Grandma was happy when they were killed. It's movie watching memories like that which make me happy I grew up when I did. When I saw it again in my 20s it still held up just as good, and finally when I got the DVD when I was in my late 30s, it still held up. It's nice to see a made-for-TV movie from the '70s still have the bite it had back then. Sometimes nostalgia is a lying bitch and sometimes it isn't...the latter is what we fans live for.

Okay, now for the big thing we all love about Halloween: C A N D Y! It was a whole different ball game when I was a kid. It would start early in the day with the class Halloween party where you would get candy and all kinds of homemade yummies that the moms of us kids would make—you could easily tell the rich moms who had too much time on their hands from the ones who were poor and would just bring a bag a candy. Either way it was a hell of a way to start things out; my mother would make chocolate Rice Krispie treats...and good god, were they yummy!

After that we would get home and eat dinner and do our homework as fast as we could so we could get to the main event. For most of the '70s, my sis was all about Kiss so she was Ace Frehley for two or three years. Me, I wore the cheap plastic costumes we all wore as kids—I'm going with me as the Road Runner, because I couldn't find a Wile E. Coyote costume—but I was all dressed. We went to my grandmother's, got candy there, and then picked up with the rest of us kids so we could go on a pillage and raid for candy!

I mean real candy. Full candy bars, cupcakes, cookies...the kind of stuff you can't give out today. Our first big stop was Mamma Morton, who I talked about earlier, but the second one was a magnificent bastard. When you got to his yard he had five scarecrows, from the bottom of the road to his front porch, all dressed the same, and he would be hiding in one of them and you never would know which one it was. So you would walk to his house never knowing where he was hiding until he jumped up and grabbed you. I won't lie...the year he stopped because he got sick we were all sad. Thank you, Scary Scarecrow Guy.

So it's the end of the night. We get home and I see my mom and dad get these predatory looks on their faces...and unlike my sis, I knew to hide my candy from the thieving bastages. Because if you left it out you would wake up with a lot of the good stuff missing. But that was after the barter-and-trade session me and my sis had in order to get candy we like and dump the stuff we didn't like. In the old days it would take you a month to get through it all with gum and Smarties going last. *Mmmm...Smarties.*

For my generation as teens, Halloween was all about the video stores and renting some scary movies to cap off our night. For the now-30s generation, it's all *Saw* and *Scream* entries, and for the now-20s generation it's the *Paranormal Activity* films. In the end it doesn't matter what tradition you have as long as you have one. So be ye young or small, wide or tall, *Happy Halloween to y'all!*

As usual, the hour is late and the candy bowl is empty; the movies have all been rented and it's time for us to watch them. So goodbye for now, and always remember to keep scanning the aisles!

BOOKSHELF

The Illustrated History of Don Post Studios

Written by Lee Lambert
Blacksparrow Auctions, 2014, USA.
Cover Price: $50

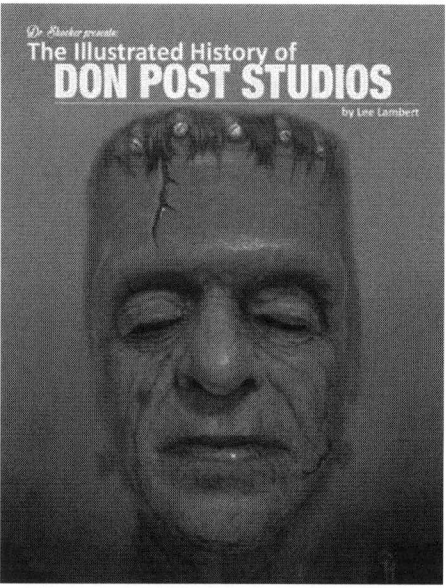

In the recent Halloween issue of *Monster!* (#10, October 2014), I took a nostalgic look back at the Don Post Studios, the famous manufacturers of latex masks whose prestigious and Hollywood operations lasted from 1938 to 2012, gaining particular prominence during the Monster Kid craze of the 1960s and early '70s, with their line of quality masks based on the classic Universal monsters. Just after completing that article, this mammoth new tome landed with a resounding *thud!* on my crypt's doorstep, and instantly had my jaw dropping from first page to last. It's a wonderful and loving salute to a period which many monster lovers of the baby boomer generation hold so special, even if the closest they ever got to the actual masks was drooling over the ads for them in the back pages of *Famous Monsters of Filmland* (and of course, *Famous Monsters* had used Don Post masks on the covers of its first two issues, as well as on the Christmas issue of its short-lived sister magazine, *Monster World*).

Authored by Lee Lambert, *The Illustrated History of Don Post Studios* clocks in at nearly 500 thick glossy pages, and as its title suggests, it tells its story from a primarily visual viewpoint. Text is very minimal, with even important decades like the 1960s covered within a handful of written pages. Thankfully, this limited text still manages to provide some nice anecdotes and a concise summary of the decade in question. These introductory essays to each chapter are then followed by a smorgasbord of photos representing the relevant period. And here, the photos are clearly able to say much more than mere words ever could. Illustrated in both color and black & white, often with one image to a single page, we are treated to a stunning array of rare photographs, many of course of the masks themselves (taken both then and now), but also a tremendous amount of behind-the-scenes production shots, vintage catalogues, correspondence and other sales material, private snaps, original 8x10 promo stills of the infamous "calendar" line of monster masks, and much, much more. The *Star Wars* and sci-fi days of the late 1970s and '80s are well-represented, and even the company's sad final days are captured through a series of photos depicting the mask molds being packed-up and shipped-off to Texas (where some have made their way to auction or into the hands of private collectors).

As spectacular as the coverage of the classic monster masks is, it is some of the more off-beat inclusions that provide many of the book's highlights for me, including the infamous Tor Johnson mask (the company's all-time best seller), and the Ray Dennis Steckler/Cash Flagg mask (a glow-in-the-dark number which was sent out to cinemas for the ushers to scare the hell out of kids sitting through Steckler's 1964 low-budget wonder **THE THRILL KILLERS**—though usually it would be the usher who ended up faring the worse). I also really enjoyed the photos of the masks making mid-1960s promotional appearances at Unimart stores (often accompanied by the likes of *Famous Monsters* editor Forry Ackerman and Tor Johnson himself), as well as the various prototypes of unproduced designs (what a pity the amazing bloody pig's head mask from **MOTEL HELL** [1980] never saw production due to the studio's closure). And I find it perfectly surreal that one of the company's last masks to hit the shelves was of the great bug-eyed title character from Lar-

ry Buchanan's 1966 late-night psychotronic wonder **CURSE OF THE SWAMP CREATURE**.

Published by Blacksparrow Auctions and presented by Dr. Shocker (a.k.a. actor/horror host/super collector Daniel Roebuck), *The Illustrated History of Don Post Studios* is, with its $50 price tag, probably not something that the casual fan is likely to pick up (and if you live outside the U.S., you could be forking out another $50+ in postage). But for anyone with a deep affection for its subject, or for budding mask sculptors and make-up effects artists, not to mention collectors of vintage monster memorabilia, this treasure trove is essential.

Launched at the Mask Fest in Indianapolis on September the 5th of this year, you can order *The Illustrated History of Don Post Studios* directly from the book's website at: *www.donpostbook.com*.

~ *John Harrison*

ABOUT THE CONTRIBUTORS...

James Bickert – was raised by finger-banging alcoholic mosquitoes in the swamp-filled drive-ins of Southeastern Georgia. He is currently working on **FRANKENSTEIN CREATED BIKERS**, the follow-up to his 2012 exploitation feature **DEAR GOD NO!**

Stephen R. Bissette – a pioneer graduate of the Joe Kubert School, currently teaches at the Center for Cartoon Studies and is renowned for *Swamp Thing*, *Taboo* (launching *From Hell* and *Lost Girls*), *"1963"*, *Tyrant*, co-creating John Constantine, and creating the world's second "24-Hour Comic" (invented by Scott McCloud for Bissette). He writes, illustrates, and has co-authored many books; his latest includes *Teen Angels & New Mutants* (2011), the short story "Copper" in *The New Dead* (2010), and he illustrated *The Vermont Monster Guide* (2009). His latest ebooks are *Bryan Talbot: Dreams & Dystopias* and the *Best of Blur* duo, *Wonders! Millennial Marvel Movies* and *Horrors! Cults, Crimes, & Creepers*.

Joe Deagnon – has been publishing comics since the late '80s beginning with the five-issue underground series *Paranoid Tales of Neurosis*. His work on *Paranoid* has been described as Harvey Pekar meets Ralph Steadman and dubbed "A *Mad* magazine for the '90s". A regular contributor to the music weekly *Exclaim*, *Film Threat* and various counter-culture 'zines in the '90s, he ended up moving his creative endeavors online with the passing of the new millennium, though he refuses to give up on the idea that print is dead. Currently, he is producing the comic series called *Chicken Outfit* with co-writer Kirby Stasyna (*Naked News*).

Steve Fenton – prefers to remain as much of a mystery to others as he is to himself.

Kris Gilpin – grew up in Florida (hated it), went to L.A. for 22 years, has an IMDb.com page, interviewed/wrote for many film 'zines during the '80s (he's in last year's great *Xerox Ferox* book) and is now still trying to find personal happiness, this time in the Midwest. Check out his crosswords by searching "Kris Gilpin" at *bestcrosswords.com*.

Brian Harris – has written for *Ultra Violent* magazine, *Exploitation Retrospect*, *Serial Killer* magazine, *Gorezone* magazine (UK) and *Hacker's Source* magazine. He's written nine books, four of which are still available, five are out-of-print. Brian has also run several websites including Joe Horror, Wildside Cinema, CineKult and Box Set Beatdown.

John Harrison – is a Melbourne-based freelance writer who has contributed chapters to the true crime books *Death Cults*, *Bad Cop Bad Cop* and *Guns, Death, Terror*, as well as writing for such publications as *Monster!* digest, *Fatal Visions*, *Cult Movies*, *Is It Uncut?*, *Filmink*, *Crime Factory*, *Headpress Journal*, *Scary Monsters* and *Bachelor Pad*, and penning reviews and liner notes for many DVD and VHS releases from Something Weird Video. In 2011, his book on vintage adult paperbacks, *Hip Pocket Sleaze*, was published by Headpress in the UK. In 2013, he self-published *Blood on the Windscreen*, a booklet which examined the violent and notorious Driver's Education films produced in America between 1959-1975. He is currently working on several fiction and non-fiction projects, and recently published a compendium of his late-'90s fanzine *Reel Wild Cinema*!

Eric Messina – can be found grinding out exploitation reviews for *theaterofguts.com* under the moniker Crankenstein. Theater of Guts was started in an effort to bring attention to the legacy of Chas Balun and *Deep Red* Magazine. The goal of the site is to review all of the titles in the VHS Bootleg catalog; past writers from *DR* have been interviewed and contributed reviews. He currently resides in Oakland Ca, with his wife Ami and dog Jack. TOG has a YouTube channel of parody trailers and video interviews, so check it out at Trailers That Smell Skunkape.

Christos Mouroukis – was born in Italy and has an MA in Feature Film from Goldsmiths University of London. He has directed award-winning and internationally broadcasted short films. His filmography on IMDb is incomplete, but the one on Wikipedia is not. He writes about genre movies in Greek (at *horrorant.com*) and English (for *Weng's Chop* and *Cinema Head Cheese*, and *Monster!*). He lives with his girlfriend Faye, and their cats Arte and Franco.

George Pacheco – has been writing professionally for well over a decade, working his way in the music industry as a fanzine editor and freelance scribe before graduating to contributing editor for the legendary *Metal Maniacs* magazine. George continues to write about music for such publications as *Outburn* and *Zero Tolerance* (UK) while focusing these days on film writing for *Weng's Chop*, *Rue Morgue*, *Video Watchdog* and the website 10kBullets.

Louis Paul – has written for numerous fanzines and published his own, *Blood Times* (87-93). He has written several books including *Inferno Italia – Der Italienische Horrorfilm* (Bertler, Lieber, '98); *Serien Morden* (Bertler, Lieber, '00); *Film Fatales – Women in Espionage Films & Television 63-73* (McFarland, '02); *Italian Horror Film Directors* (McFarland, '05, '10); and *Tales from the Cult Film Trenches – Interviews with 36 Actors from Horror, Science Fiction and Exploitation Cinema* (McFarland, '07). Louis blames a 42nd Street double-bill of Umberto Lenzi's **ALMOST HUMAN** and the 3D porno **HARD CANDY** (with John Holmes) for disturbing his psyche for life.

Tim Paxton – has been publishing stuff about monsters since 1979, and currently lives to write about fantastic cinema from India. He is even considering publishing a book on the subject. What a knucklehead.

David Reddick – works full-time for Jim Davis at the "Garfield" studio as a cartoonist and Digital/Social Media Coordinator. He also creates his own worldwide-syndicated comic strip *Intelligent Life*, distributed by King Features Syndicate to newspapers and online (*www.IntelligentLifeComics.com*), and is the creator/writer/artist of the highly-popular *Star Trek* webcomic *The Trek Life*, which ran for three years at the official *Star Trek* website *StarTrek.com*. He has also been the cartoonist behind *Gene's Journal* and *Rod & Barry*, two popular webcomics which ran for five years at the official Roddenberry Entertainment website at *Roddenberry.com*. He is also the creator of the highly-popular fantasy webcomic *Legend of Bill*, which has been running for more than five years, and has a legion of dedicated fans.

Steven Ronquillo – is a pretentious know-it-all who looks down on his fellow film fans and refuses to reveal his faves to them unless it makes him look good.

Art Stevenson – has been film-obsessed since he first encountered **STAR TREK II: THE WRATH OF KHAN** and failed to successfully build a replica of the Enterprise NCC-1701-A out of Legos. Committed tea drinker. He spends his days in traditional old England, or Tolkien's real-life Mordor, attempting to raise money for an expedition to the planet mistakenly named "Mars" (in fact, Tatooine). He plans by "the year of our Lord 2020" to lead an expedition to find and excavate the sites of George Lucas' **STAR WARS**, which he hopes to fund through his film writing. Art now resides in exile in the UK after a defense of an American suburban neighborhood went awry. He would challenge Dana Olsen to a cage fight, but due to the moral implications, instead directs all his anger towards **THE 'BURBS** director Joe Dante who he blames for everything that goes wrong…Damn it, Joe!

Tony Strauss – has been writing about cinema in print and online for nearly two decades. His existence as that rarest and most annoying of creatures—an artsy-fartsy movie snob who loves trash cinema (yes, it's possible)—often leaves him as the odd man out in both intellectual and lowbrow film discussions. Most movies that people describe as "boring" or "confusing" enthrall him, while the kinds of movies that are described as "non-stop action" usually bore him to tears. He has a BFA in Film, but don't hold that against him.

Salvatore Tarantola – is an artist born, raised, and currently living in Brooklyn, NY. His influences include Wally Wood, Crumb, and Moebius. He loves Japanese sci-fi and Hammer films.

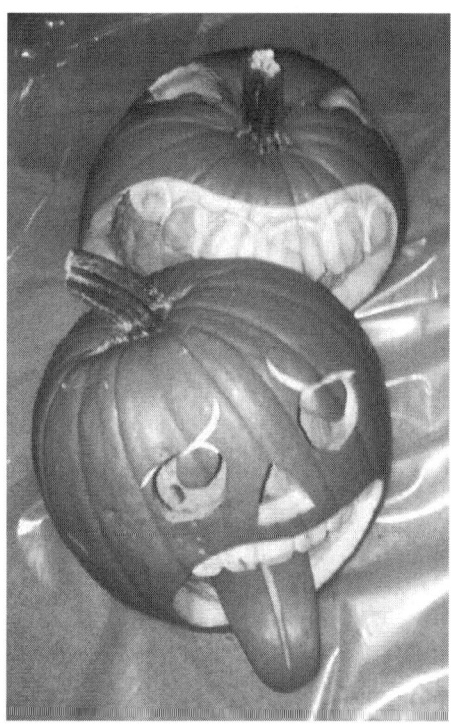

Printed in Great Britain
by Amazon.co.uk, Ltd.,
Marston Gate.